JAZZ DANCE &
JAZZ GYMNASTICS
By Uta Fischer–Munstermann

1

JAZZ DANCE
&
JAZZ GYMNASTICS
including disco dancing

By Uta Fischer—Munstermann

Introduction by Liz Williamson
Edited and adapted by Liz Williamson

STERLING PUBLISHING CO., INC. **NEW YORK**
Oak Tree Press Co., Ltd. London & Sydney

Other Books of Interest

Aqua-Rhythmics
Dancing Games for Children of All Ages
Girls' Gymnastics
Gymnastics
Movement Games for Children of All Ages
Musical Games for Children of All Ages
Olympic Gymnastics
Singing and Dancing Games for the Very Young
Tumbling and Trampolining
Yoga for Kids

Translated by Dale S. Cunningham
Photos by Rupert Leser
Diagrams by Guntram Herold

Second Printing, 1979
Copyright © 1978
Sterling Publishing Co., Inc.
Two Park Avenue, New York, N.Y.
10016

Originally published in German under
the title
"Von der Jazzgymnastik zum Jazz-
tanz"

Copyright © 1975 Pohl-Verlag
3100 Celle, West Germany.

Distributed in Australia by Oak Tree
Press Co. Ltd.
P.O. Box J34, Brickfield Hill, Sydney
2000, NSW.

Distributed in the United Kingdom
by Ward Lock Ltd.,
116 Baker Street, London W.1

Manufactured in the United States
of America

Library of Congress Catalog Card
No: 78-57794
Sterling ISBN 0-8069- 4618-0 Trade
4620-2 Paper
4619-9 Library
Oak Tree 7061-2601-7
2602-5

Table of Contents

2

3

Introduction

Introduction

Jazz! What is this provocative, elusive dance called Jazz?

Jazz dance was born in America of African parents. Its prehistory was recorded in drumbeats, nothing more permanent. It came out of the earliest sounds of Africa – thump, thump, thump. An internal sound. Regular, pace-setting, the beat of the heart.

Jazz is so rich that it intimidates some people. They want to know, "Is this jazz? Is that jazz?" It all is jazz – since jazz dance has taken on many guises in its never-ending search for acceptability. It is Broadway show dance, movie musical dance. You see it on television shows and on the concert stage, in Las Vegas nightclubs and in discotheques.

All over the world, interest in jazz dance is burgeoning. More students than ever are studying jazz forms. Teachers, performers – everyone – all are eager to find out more about this rich branch of the arts. The audience for jazz dance increases each year. And the misconceptions and preconceptions that people have about jazz dance are myriad.

The very word "jazz" causes trouble for some. It baffles people who must have neat definitions. The usually authoritative *Oxford English*

Dictionary says that the origin of the word is "unknown: generally said to be Negro." Jazz dance it goes on, is a "kind of ragtime dance (3 beats to 4 musical notes), introduced from the United States to Europe towards the end of 1918."

Of course, jazz dance has a history previous to its introduction to Europe. The *American Heritage Dictionary* defines jazz as "a kind of native American music first played extemporaneously by Negro bands in Southern towns at the turn of the century and in most styles having a strong but flexible rhythmic understructure with solo and ensemble improvisations on basic tunes and chord patterns, and, in more recent styles, a highly sophisticated harmonic idiom."

In 1920 a monograph called *All About the Latest Dances* described early bands "jazzing" a tune: "That is to say, they slur the notes, they syncopate, and each instrument puts in a lot of fancy bits of its own."

They are all right, but incomplete. Basically, jazz dance is an approach. It is ever-changing, but vitality is a constant. No movement is dull. There is an unabated theatricality about it. No motion is perfunctory. Improvisation is the core.

Jazz dance and music are indigenous American art forms, tracing to Africa. Uprooted to America, the black slave had a different life. The African drum was prohibited, except in Louisiana and coastal Georgia. The ritual African dance was also prohibited. But rhythm continued and dance continued. If you have no drum, you can still strike a rhythm by moving your foot through the dirt on the ground – the origin of sand dance. You can clap; you can make rhythmic noises with your voice.

Many famous black dancers of the early years of the 20th century began their careers dancing on the streets for pennies and nickels thrown by passers-by. The blacks were not allowed to perform the dances on stage. Many black performers became embittered and migrated to Europe, introduced jazz dance and music, and found immediate acceptance and enthusiasm.

Jazz dance has etched out its own niche in the fine arts. Jazz choreography has encompassed social dance, the Broadway show and the Hollywood movie and become an end unto itself. Jazz dance is infectious. It's fancy. It's tricky. It's showing off your body with quirky, subtle moves, with lyrical, sustained motions, with playful, unexpected steps against a steady rhythm.

Jazz dancing is one of the most elusive types of dancing to teach. Unlike ballet, it is not a definite set of steps and movements. Unlike modern dance, it is not a specific style of movement or thinking. Whatever jazz dance is, it is different – different from other art forms – and exciting. The pace of jazz dancing is often explosive. It deals with themes as old as the oldest civilizations and as futuristic as the robot dancer, $R_2 D_2$, in the movie "Star Wars."

Jazz dance is always changing, as is jazz music. It consists at any given moment of the old and the new; the old rearranged into something new. In fact, jazz dance rearranges just about everything: the way people walk, the way they communicate, the way they touch.

Very little has been written about jazz dance to date – and practical books about it are almost non-existent – due partly to the difficulty of describing dance movements, and partly to the fact that jazz dance has barely begun to be taken seriously as an art form. With this book, Ms. Fischer-Munstermann adds a great deal that is valuable to the literature in the field. With

her extraordinarily good selection of photos of jazz dancers in action and her detailed analyses of movement, she shows what jazz dance looks like and feels like. The exercises she presents are designed to develop flexibility, strength and endurance, as well as the awareness and control necessary to all dancers.

But this is not an "exercise" book. It is a dance book – filled with practical ideas for dramatic movement and experimentation, which encourage an increasing sensitivity in the dancer and versatility of movement. The techniques have been arranged in an order that is most beneficial to the body and its needs, and it is up to you how many times you do this exercise or that one – or what kind of practice program you set up. It deals in great detail with the concept of isolation of movement of the body parts, presenting the theory that working on these movements is the only way for the jazz dancer to become completely aware of his or her body as an instrument.

The careful arrangements of patterns and exercises make the book easy to read and follow, to perform and enjoy. They follow in levels – beginner, intermediate and advanced – bringing the dancer

quite naturally to improvisation and choreography in the jazz idiom. That's what it's all about! – Technique is a means to an end – and the end product is to DANCE!

High energy – exhilaration – freedom of movement are all inherent in jazz – and this book captures that joy! So read on – learn – perform – DANCE, and delight in the fact that your body is moving well, freely, excitingly, creatively – and that you are controlling it in a knowledgeable way.

Liz Williamson
New York. 1978

4

Foreword

Foreword

Jazz dance, like jazz itself, was created by the Afro-American, and it has been developing rapidly and increasing in popularity since the 18th century. It combines genuine African dance, American modern dance, and classical European ballet. And these 3 directions blend together in jazz dance to such an extent that it is almost impossible now to identify the source of a specific technique.

No dance can exist without thoroughly preparing the "instrument of dance" – the human body. This preparation is called many things: dance gymnastics, dance training, dance technique or dance exercise. They all mean simply *practice*, just as the word *gymnastics* did originally. In this book it is called "jazz gymnastics," preparing your body for the technique, style and expression of jazz dance. Jazz dance has other important links to gymnastics, which we'll explore later.

Dance is one of the oldest human means of expression. Rhythmic movements, gestures and mimicry have been accompanied by music, drums or song and performed as dances for thousands of years.

People of practically any age and stage of development can dance.

Dancing starts when movement arises spontaneously from inner drives. These simple, basic dance forms are then shaded, varied, and combined with other forms.

Improvisation is dancing, too, regardless of the talent and ability of the improvisers. As you experiment, you translate spontaneous ideas into movement. As you learn jazz techniques and test them out, you automatically and instantly improvise.

Choreography is the final step in this creative process. The dance you put together is a well thought-out arrangement of motifs of movement. It has a lasting character as you refine it into a definite form which you can repeat. It expresses your joy of movement. And as your technical ability grows, you will be increasingly successful in injecting your own individual expression into your dancing.

Both processes – improvisation (exploring and developing combinations of movement) and choreography (pinning them down so that you can do the dance again in the exact same way) are creative processes. They complement each other. They result naturally as you use the techniques of jazz gymnastics and jazz dance.

Why Jazz?

Both jazz and disco have an ecstatic freedom about them. Jazz dance technique has been called a technique of ecstasy. Actually, many African dances express ecstasy, rapture, escape from one's self and union with God.

Obviously, ecstasy in this sense is not (necessarily) the goal of jazz dancing. But a positive kind of intoxication is part of it. In gymnastic, rhythmic dancing, you can lose yourself in spontaneous movement, in the joy of repetition, and not want to stop. This exhilaration makes you feel looser, happier, freer. Naturally, it is easier to feel that way in a dim discotheque than in a gym or your own living room. But it is primarily the dance forms, the use of the body centers, and the music which "intoxicate" you. The more intense the dance, the more completely you can surrender yourself to it. The more powerful the rhythm, the more fully you experience that intoxication.

Jazz and Gymnastics

Jazz and disco gymnastics and dance are also excellent forms of physical training. They don't replace traditional gymnastics, but rather expand and enrich it. With their special music and "jazzy" movements, they can provide gymnastics with new impulses and motivations. Jazz dance is being used increasingly by gymnasts who are developing unique and creative floorwork.

Modern music and jazz often accompany gymnastics, and not only in floorwork. Try playing jazz music when you're using hand devices, such as the rod, balls, rings and ropes, and relating your jazz movements to them. You can use the rod, for example, to illustrate directions of space and movement, counter-directions and twisting, contraction and release, as well as springs, falls and levels. You can include it as a dancing tool, the way they do it in eastern European cane dances or African weapon dances.

Jazz and Disco Dancing

Jazz dance is a concept of movement which can be called *the style of our times*. Disco is an offshoot of jazz dance, which is based, like rock and roll and the twist, on elements of African dance. Today it is danced in discotheques along with rock and other styles. Many of the same techniques used in jazz dance apply in disco, but few of the dancers have really mastered them.

Disco is bound to one area with little movement through space. The movements are performed more inside the body centers than in jazz dance. Disco has developed fixed steps, figures, and sequences – you'll see how to do the Funky-Broadway, Jingling, the Skate, the Tighten Up, the Penguin – and others later on in this book – and new ones are being added constantly. Disco is social dancing, the ballroom dancing that people are doing today, while jazz dance tends to be expressive dance, an artistic form which disco may or may not be.

Creative Jazz

If you already know many of the disco dances, why should you go on to jazz dancing? It's true that free creative jazz dancing is rarely seen in a discotheque and you'd only call attention to yourself if you did it. But through jazz gymnastics, you'll improve your disco technique, your mobility and your coordination. You'll also do some exciting dancing. Don't be afraid to try new forms, as well as the ones you already know. In this book you'll learn more disco steps, and if you go on to work creatively, you can make them richer in variation, fuller in expression and much more individual.

You can invent steps of your own in jazz and disco rhythms which you can perform anywhere – in a discotheque or on a stage. You can start with a musical theme you love, a movement that appeals to you, or an idea or an emotion. As you work through this book, you'll develop a large repertoire of movements. You'll be able to select the dance form you want and develop it in space and time.

What About Music?

Always use modern music when you practice. It helps in every part of your training – isolation technique, coordination, variations and combinations, improvisations – and jazz music is available everywhere on records and tape. Jazz music and movement are closely related. The music stimulates the movement, accompanies it, and motivates it. You interpret jazz music through movement; you translate its syncopation, dynamics, and phrasing into movement. You can use jazz and disco music, African drum rhythms and folk music as well as jazzed-up classical pieces. Always start with music; never practice the movement first without it as a "dry run." Music is the cause, not an adornment of dancing!

5

6

7

8

1 The Techniques of Jazz Dance

The Techniques of Jazz Dance

The basic techniques of jazz dance fall into 5 categories:

Isolation
Polycentrics
Tension-release
Jazz Movements
Special Movements

As you read through the book, you'll take a close look at each one of these techniques, with many practice exercises and action photographs that show not only how they work but how they *feel*. If you follow the sequences set out here, you'll try the movement patterns, experiment with them, practice them and apply them freely. As you develop your technique, you'll naturally translate them into free and unstructured dance forms by varying them, combining them and improvising with them. Finally, you'll create dances of your own.

Isolation
Moving individual parts of your body (body centers) independently of the others

In disco and jazz dance, we divide the body into individual *centers* of movement. The principal centers are:

the head   the pelvis
the shoulders   the arms
the chest   the legs

The jazz dancer needs to learn to control and use these individual parts of the body separately – to *isolate* them.

It's easy to isolate movements of your shoulders, arms, pelvis and legs. Isolated head and chest movements are more difficult and require special practice, but there are ways to master them. You'll find out how in Chapter 2.

Polycentrics
Coordinating 2 and more centers

A major task in jazz dance is working out coordinations of different body centers at the same time (*polycentrics*). These movements relate to each other, but they are in constant contrast. A complex combination may call for all the body centers to be working in *isolation* at the same time!

One rule of coordination is important: In jazz dance, your head almost always moves in the same direction as your pelvis, while your chest moves in the opposite direction. This creates a dramatic curve in your body, which leads you into typical disco and jazz positions.

Because of the intense movements you'll be making with your body, jazz technique is great physical

training. Because of the precise movements you'll be making in jazz rhythm – where 1 body center may have to move at half or twice the *tempo* of another – you'll develop a finely-tuned feeling for rhythm. Enormous demands also will be made on your coordination, which you'll be relearning on new and higher levels.

Tension-release
Relaxation, contraction, release, extension, flexion

In jazz dance, moments of tension alternate with spontaneous relaxation of your entire body or of some parts of your body.

Take a look at Chapter 4. The exercises there will help you develop a strong feeling for tension and relaxation in your own body.

Jazz dance may call for relaxation and tension simultaneously. While 1 part of your body is tense and in action, the others may be following the impulses loosely and passively. This simultaneous expression is at the essence of jazz dancing.

Jazz movements based on simple gymnastics
Walking, running, hopping, jumping

and turning (locomotor types); and those based on internal body movements – those you do without changing place, such as swinging, turning, and floor movements (levels)

Simple movements – a jazz walk, for example – can multiply within a rhythmic period. The shift of your weight from 1 foot to the other may be divided into 2 or 3 parts and sometimes into many parts. That simple jazz step consists of placing the ball of your foot on the floor without putting your weight on it at the first part of the beat. Only on the second part of the beat does your weight follow with some kind of emphasis – shaking your knee, perhaps – or accenting it with your heel (see Jazz Walks, Chapter 5).

Other simple movements get more complex when done in jazz style. Individual parts of your body may work in *opposition* to each other – 1 arm moving backward while the other moves forward, for example. Typical positions of your arms in jazz dance are angular oppositions of your elbows, hands and fingers. You might spread your fingers so that the line of your arm is even further broken up into parts. Your moving leg might be bent at the knee, drawn up, rolled in or out from your hip, and have a bent ankle. This principle of opposition

also extends the possibilities for movement and expression in jazz dance.

Special movements
Counter-movements and twisting, jazz falls, and deep levels in combinations

"Deep levels" means dancing which incorporates lying, creeping, sitting, crouching, and transitions in and out of these floor positions.

Levels are always used in connection with falls and jumps, and they frequently are acrobatic. A fall can be a continuous flowing movement in which you start out standing, walking, running or jumping and go through kneeling to sitting, ending up lying on the floor. Or it can move with hesitation and sudden stops.

When you practice falls and levels, work on them gradually as flowing combinations. Practice difficult falls on mats and with the aid of a partner. After you master the movements, you can put them into rhythmic patterns very rapidly and adapt them to music.

As you work your way through this book, you'll be discovering individual forms and creating your own variations on them. You'll also

learn certain "basic forms" – steps – routines which you can use to build on.

Many of these combinations are dynamic "show" pieces, wonderfully effective in performance. They are fun to do because of their "crazy" effect, and mastering the acrobatic aspects of the dance is especially satisfying. It's an unbeatable combination.

9

10

2 Isolation: Training the Centers of Movement

Movement Patterns, Practice Patterns, Movement Combinations

Isolation: Training the Centers of Movement

Movement Patterns, Practice Patterns, Movement Combinations

Isolation technique means training your centers of movement. The independent mobility of the major centers – your head, shoulders, chest, pelvis, arms and legs – is an important part of jazz dance.

Head Movements

Movement Patterns

1. Explore the possibilities for moving your head.

2. Shake your head loosely, swing it, rotate it, and move it suddenly.

3. Move your head in small nodding or shaking movements while dancing in place.

4. Move your head in movements which are as large as possible, including your upper back in the movement.

5. Bend your upper body forward loosely. Then move it backward or to the side, with your head hanging in the same direction.

6. Place your feet parallel to each other—and about a foot apart (called second position in ballet); for convenience' sake we'll call this

a *straddle* position. Hop rapidly, so that the vibrations run through your entire body to your head.

7. Practice various head movements as you walk across the room.

11

Practice Patterns

Perform the following exercises standing in a relaxed position or sitting cross-legged (like a tailor) with shoulders hanging loosely.

1. Head Nodding

Start with your head in a center position and move it forward, center, back, center. Start with a soft nodding movement and then change to a rapid nodding movement.

2. Head Tipping

Move your head toward the right, then center; toward the left, then center. When you go toward the side, put your ear to your shoulder with your shoulders drawn up.

Do the same thing with dropped shoulders.

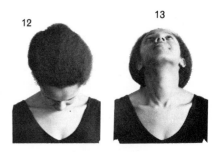

12   13

14   15

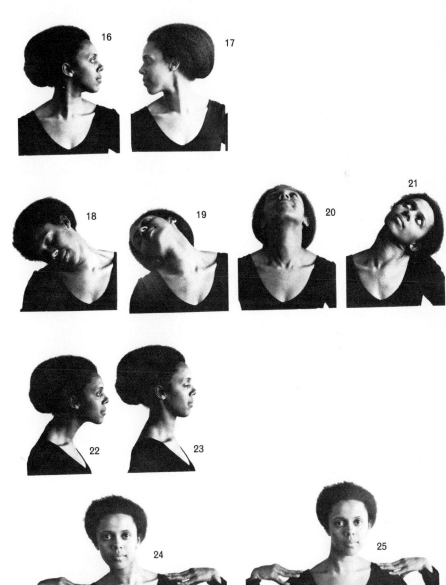

3. Head Turning
Starting from the center, turn to the right, then center; to the left, then center. Turn as far as possible, but do it smoothly, not with a jerk.

4. Head Rotating
Rotate your head, starting toward the front, then to the left and right, moving your head all the way down to your collarbone.

Make half circles to the rear (bend your head backward at the nape of your neck).

Now do 1½ head rotations in each direction. Then change direction, first to a count of 4 and then to a count of 2.

5. Head shifting

Shift your head forward and draw it back.

Shift your head toward the left and right on a single level (as in exotic Indian dances).

Movement Combinations

1. Head Nodding

As you do this, dip with your knees (illus. 26), emphasizing the stretching movement (see illus. 27). Do the same thing as you shift your weight to your right leg and then your left leg. Repeat the same movements, finishing with a hop.

2. Head Tipping

As you do this, move your right leg to the side and draw it up. Then do the same with your left leg.

Move your head and leg in the same direction.

3. Head Turning

Walk forward with a long-stride step. Turn your head to the left and right while you walk (illus. 28 and 29). Swing your arms out like pendulums (stretch them as you swing), alternating with your steps. Do the same thing with a quiet jumping run (a type of jazz run—illus. 30).

4. Head Rotating

In straddle position, make deeper circles with your head so that your whole body is involved, swinging your head to the right and back to the left. Shift your weight as you do this (illus. 31).

Make 1½ head circles, but this time, move your feet, too. Step to the right, to the side, forward, to the side, and rotate your head in the direction that you are moving.

Do the same thing to the left.

Now, as you circle your head to the right, accent the movement as you fall forward (illus. 32). Bend your chest slightly forward and to the side. Bend your knees slightly, too. Circle with your head 3 times in succession with increasing momentum. Include your body in the movement from the waist up. Bend your knees (illus. 33 and 34).

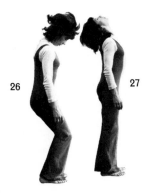

26   27

28

29

30

Shoulder Movements

Movement Patterns

1. Move your shoulders while you lie on your back. Try out all the possibilities for shoulder movements from that position.

2. Still lying on your back, work your way into new positions, starting from impulses from your shoulders. Try it lying on your side.

3. Try the same thing kneeling. There are more possibilities for movement from this position. Let your arms hang loose, following the impulses from your shoulders.

4. Let your whole body move along with your shoulders.

With a partner

5. Kneel facing each other and try to make shoulder contact.

6. Mirror-image exercise:
One of the partners initiates the shoulder movements; the other does them as a mirror image.

Try the same thing standing, making larger movements upward, down and to the sides.

Put these patterns together with steps and move in space.

Practice Patterns

Try these passively, first with your arms hanging loosely and then while holding out your arms at shoulder level.

1. Raise and lower your shoulders from a central position (illus. 35): Raise, center; lower deeply, center. Do this as an angular movement, first slowly, then more rapidly (illus. 36).

Move your shoulders in opposite directions, one at a time. As you lift your right shoulder, simultaneously lower your left shoulder (illus. 37).

Lift and drop your shoulders one after the other—marionette-like.

2. Move your shoulders forward and backward. Do this with your arms low and to the side.

Do it with your arms extended, palms facing forward.

First practice both shoulders moving back and forth together and then move them in opposition to each other (illus. 38).

3. Forward and Backward Shoulder Circles

Do half circles upward and then half circles downward.

Do full shoulder circles and figure 8's.

4. Turn your shoulders in and out. While you do it, stretch your arms out to the side and turn them so that your palms are facing upward (illus. 40).

Round your back and roll your shoulders backward in turn as you do it (illus. 39 and 40).

5. Do the exercise with your hands stretched to the side, palms facing forward. Draw back, starting from your shoulder blades (illus. 41 and 42).

6 Trace a half circle—from the top forward—with your shoulder blades. While you do it, keep the palms of your hands stretched more or less forward. Your elbows are now in an angular position (illus. 43).

Do the same thing in reverse.

When you first try this pattern, you may want to place the palms of your hands on a wall.

Movement Combinations

1. Spring up twice onto the ball of your right foot and twice onto the ball of your left foot. Keep your shoulders relaxed, lifting and dropping them as you move, first together and then in opposition to each other.

Repeat the same thing while you move forward, actively shaking your shoulders.

2. Turn to the side in straddle position. Turn your shoulders forward and backward, first together, then one at a time. As you do it, lean your upper body backward (illus. 44).

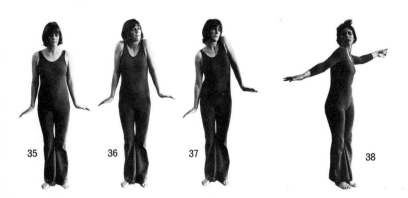

35   36   37   38

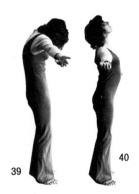

39   40

41

42

43

Practice this with a high walk, a low walk, and walking forward (limbo style). See illus. 44–46.

Practice it with shoulder circles, as you move forward, backward, and to the side.

3. Do the same thing with lifted forearms, your palms facing forward or upward, and making circles with your elbows.

4. Take steps forward, backward and sideways. As you do it, turn your shoulders in and out, with your arms stretched out to the sides.

5. Rotate your shoulders in and out in opposing movements (twisting). Shift your chest from right to left as you twist (illus. 47).

6. Connect your shoulder twisting with diagonal steps, crossing your feet and moving from side to side (illus. 48).

Chest Movements

Now you'll be moving your chest in isolation, starting from your waist. These are small, very precise movements, so it's important to start them at the right spot.

Movement Patterns

1. Sit on a bench or on the floor with criss-crossed legs (tailor-style). Try to move your chest from the waist upwards. This is easier to do when your pelvis is fixed in 1 spot as it is when you're sitting.

2. Explore the pattern to see what movements are possible—forward, backward—circles to the left and right. Usually, forward-backward movements are easier. Movements to the side are more unusual. Get to feel how they start, and it's easier to learn to do them.

3. With your side close to a wall, hold your arms behind your head, with your forearms against each other in such a way that your hands grasp your elbows. Try to touch the wall with sideways movements of your chest.

With a partner

4. Practice doing sideways movements of your chest in front of a mirror or in front of a window (illus. 49 and 50).

44

45

46

47

48

53

5. Draw you right arm all the way to the left across your chest, while you shift the right side of your chest to the right. These are opposing movements. Do it to the other side (illus. 53).

6. Practice with a partner who is standing next to you. Try to make contact moving sideways with your chest.

7. Face your partner. Clasp right hands, and draw each other in opposite directions, so that the right side of your chest moves in an arc toward the right.

Change hands smoothly and pull to the other side.

8. Do the same thing standing back-to-back. Clasp hands over your head. Pull to each side.

9. Stand in front of a wall (or a mirror or a window), facing it, and try to touch it by moving your chest forward (illus. 51 and 52).

10. Try the same thing back-to-back with a partner. Feel which muscles are needed (illus. 54).

11. Place your hands on your knees, as you stand in a slightly bent straddle position (illus. 55). Then alternately press your chest forward and backward.

12. Do the same thing, allowing your pelvis to move along with your chest (illus. 56).

13. Now do the same thing, but include your head. This will be a contraction-release movement.

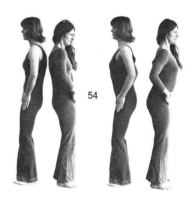

54

49

50

51

52

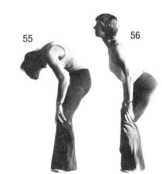

55

56

14. Combination: Move your chest in a square, forward, to the right, backward, to the left.

15. Let your chest trace a circle. Do it slowly at first, counting to 4, and then faster, counting to 2. Practice this in place.

Movement Combinations

1. Combine the forward-backward movement of your chest with arm movements, while standing. For example:

Shift your chest forward, holding your arms at your side, and press the palms of your hands out to the side.

Hold your chest in a central position, your arms out in front of it. Draw your chest back, as you move your arms forward together at shoulder height. Press your palms forward (illus. 58).

2. Connect the forward movement of your chest with stepping forward, and of drawing your chest back with stepping back.

As you do this, hold your arms horizontally at shoulder height and move them back and forth (in directions opposite to those of your chest). See illus. 57.

Include your head in the overall movement.

Do it with a partner, alternately moving toward and away from each other.

Change your direction in space by adding quarter or half turns.

With a group

Two groups could move toward each other, for example, or 1 dancer could stand in front of a group, leading the movement.

Pelvic Isolation

Movement Patterns

1. Try doing a belly dance, letting the center of your body (your pelvis or hips) lead you, providing the impulse for dancing. (Belly dances are found all over the world, not only in the Middle East, but on the Pacific Islands, in Africa and in Latin America.)

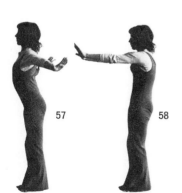

57   58

59

2. At first, let the rest of your body and your upper thighs follow along.

3. Examine the movements of your pelvis. In what directions can it move? Which are difficult? Which are easy?

4. Try out soft, round, flowing movements with your pelvis. While you explore them, take steps and turn in place (illus. 59).

5. Shake your hips impulsively in various directions. As you finish a sequence of these sharp shakes, allow your feet to leave the floor momentarily (hop).

With a partner or a group

6. Stand close to each other and move your hips in the same direction and with the same tempo.

7. Try the same thing standing *very* close together (illus. 61).

Note: Wild, broad, ranging movements will lead to finer, isolated pelvic movements. Repeat these exercises and work on improving the precise isolation technique.

Practice Patterns

Practice pelvic movements in a straddle position.

1. Pelvic Movement to the Sides

Shift your pelvis from center, first to the right, then to the left.

2. Hip Lift

Place your right toes next to your left foot and lift your hip until your right leg is extended.

Let your hip drop, and bend your right knee slightly forward. Keep your left leg straight.

60

61

30

Switch legs and practice this
exercise at a rapid tempo.

3. Pelvic Tip

Tip your pelvis so far forward that
you form a hollow with your back.
Straighten your pelvis. Your lower
back will be slightly rounded. Tip
and straighten up, in rhythm
(illus. 60).

4. Pelvic Circles

This is a combination of forward,
backward and sideways movements.
Move your pelvis sharply toward
the right, backward, toward the
left and forward, in a rectangle.

Practice these round pelvic circles
in both directions. Keep the pelvic
movement as isolated as possible.
Try not to move your legs or chest
along with it.

Movement Combinations

1. Combine 1 of these pelvic
movements with steps.

2. Which pelvic movement goes
best with those steps? The
sideways pelvic movement, for
example, works well with steps
forward and sideways, crossing
your feet as you go. The forward
and backward movement of your

62

pelvis is easy to do on the balls of your feet with your knees bent (illus. 64).

3. Explore other types of walking (jazz walks) and combine them with hip movements.

4. Move your pelvis *with* your steps first, and then opposite to them. Different types of walking will result (see Jazz Walks, Chapter 5).

5. Try out steps with half and full pelvic circles.

6. Make impulsive hip movements walking diagonally across the room.

7. Coordinate sideways movements of your head with sideways movements of your pelvis, each going in the same direction.

Combine the same movements walking sideways and making cross steps.

8. Moving diagonally across the room, do hip lifts with quick impulses. As you do them, take short steps forward or sideways— 3 times in 1 direction, then changing directions on the 4th beat.

9. Practice tipping and straightening your pelvis while shifting your weight from your left to your right leg (illus. 63-65).

Do the same thing going low with a bent knee and high on the ball of your foot as you tip.

10. Practice pelvic circles with head circles in the same direction and with the same tempo.

You'll find many more possibilities in the section on Jazz Walks in Chapter 5.

Isolating Your Back

A wave movement starts from your pelvis and passes through your lower back, your upper back, and on through your neck.

Movement Patterns

1. On your hands and knees on the floor raise and lower your back: First arch your back like a cat (illus. 66); then lower it, horseback-style (illus. 67). Start with your lower back and let the movement run all the way through your spine to your head.

Practice this with music that starts

63

64

65

slowly and then gets fast and intense, until you are shaking.

Practice slowly against the resistance provided by a partner who presses with his or her fingertips against your individual vertebrae, 1 after the other, from bottom to top. Really round your back as your partner presses (illus. 66).

2. Standing, place both your hands on a bar (or a floating beam, ballet barre, or your partner) with your upper body bent horizontally. Raise and lower your back in this position just as you did in Pattern #1. Get your partner to help by pressing against your back, as before.

3. Standing upright, let the impulse move from your pelvis right up your back in a slow smooth wave.

4. Do the same thing, finishing with a quick hop, your upper body bent forward. Each hop is an impulse which runs rapidly through your back to your head.

Combine the wave with the swinging and circling of your arms. As you do it, lightly spring up and down (without your feet leaving the ground).

5. Standing bent with your back parallel to the floor, take steps forward or diagonally. As you

walk, let 1 or 2 wave impulses run through your back.

Make 1 wave movement per step. You can hold your head calmly, or include it in the movement.

With a group

6. Two or 4 dancers stand in a row behind each other with their backs parallel to the floor, holding each other at the hips. They all move their backs up and down in the same rhythm. They can also do the movement 1 after another, so that their backs rise and sink like waves. It's a great group effect!

66

67

3 Polycentrics in Jazz Dance

Movement Coordinations in Disco & Jazz

Polycentrics in Jazz Dance

Movement Coordinations in Disco and Jazz

Polycentric movements proceed simultaneously from several body centers – head, shoulders, chest, pelvis, arms, legs. This is jazz movement. In traditional dance, the impulse to move starts from a single body center and is transmitted to your entire body. In disco and jazz dancing, as well, your entire body is involved in intense movement, but the impulse to move comes not from only 1 center, but from several of them at the same time.

This is something new, something unusual – coordination of different centers of movement. After you have mastered the techniques of isolation and can move these centers independently of each other, you are ready to practice them in combination: first the interplay of 2 centers, then 3, and then more. All the examples will start with the pelvis as the main center of motion, and add the remaining centers 1 at a time.

Play disco music, jazz, or African drum rhythms while you practice.

You may recognize some of the following coordinations. They are disco combinations:
The Horse, the Funky-Broadway, Jingling, the Penguin, the Skate, and Tighten Up.

The Horse

Practice Patterns for Sideways Pelvic Movement (see illus. 69)

1. With sideways movements of your chest

Move your pelvis toward the left and your chest toward the right: your upper body will slant to the side as you do this.

Do this, taking swaying steps in place – or simply shifting your weight from foot to foot.

Do the same thing with short steps sideways: Lead with your

69

pelvis in the direction of your movement, as your chest pulls in the opposite direction.

Now do it again, but this time move your chest in the direction of movement, and let your pelvis pull in the opposite direction.

Now do this with cross-steps 4 times in 1 direction, then changing direction.

2. With sideways movements of your head

Stand in straddle position in place, and make sideways pelvic

movements as you tip your head sideways toward your pelvis.

Each time, move your head and your pelvis toward each other, so that your back will be curved toward the side.

Do the same thing sideways and with cross-steps.

3. Overall sideways coordination

Combine the pelvic, chest and head centers, and you're doing the "Horse."

4. Explore variations on this basic step.

The Funky-Broadway

Practice Patterns for Tipping Your Pelvis (illus. 72)

1. Pelvis and Chest

While tipping your pelvis forward, arch your chest forward so that your back is sharply curved. Now do the opposite: Straighten your pelvis and move your chest backward, to form a rounded back.

Move flowingly from 1 position to the other, and include your head in the movement.

2. Pelvis and Shoulders

Move your pelvis forward and backward. With your arms hanging loosely, move your shoulders forward and backward in a semi-circle, parallel to your pelvis.

Practice this forward and backward movement of your pelvis and shoulders in a smooth, flowing way.

3. Pelvis, Arms and Shoulders

Swing your arms back and forth from your shoulders as you move your pelvis forward and backward.

As you circle your shoulders forward, extend your arms and

70   71

72

swing them back past your upper
thighs into a stretched position
to the rear and slightly out to
the side.

As you make the semi-circle toward
the back with your shoulders, angle
your arms forward at the elbows.
Your hands will finish at shoulder
height with your palms facing
forward.

Combine the arm swings with the
movement of your pelvis. Your
arms will be stretched far backward
when your pelvis is tipped forward.
At the point where your pelvis is
straight, your arms swing through
toward the forward position high
or low (this is the *funky* arm
movement).

4. Pelvis and Head

Move your head in the same
direction as your pelvis. Your
pelvis will move forward at the
same time that your head is forward (chin on your chest). Move
your pelvis back and lean your
head back from the nape of your
neck. Practice these movements
in a smooth flow.

5. Overall Coordination

The combination of your head,
shoulders, chest and pelvis,
moving forward and backward

result in a continuous wave
movement vertically through your
entire body. This is the disco step
called the "Funky-Broadway."

6. Funky Variations

Bend your knees and then stretch
in place (intensifying the low-high
movement).

Shift your weight to the right and
left with the low-high movements.

Take sideways crossed steps or
short forward or diagonal steps
in the funky movement.

Practice the funky movement
walking on the balls of your feet,
with deep knee bends.

Make additional arm movements,
both arms moving at the same
time together or alternately.

Tighten Up and The Penguin

Practice Exercises for the Hip Lift (illus. 73)

1. Pelvis and Head

Standing, place the tip of your
right foot next to your left. Raise
and lower your right hip to the
right. As you do this, tip your head
toward your raised hip, and back.

Do the same thing toward the left.

Do it in loose rapid movements,
with a 2-count.

As you do it, let your forearms
hang down loosely, moving in
opposite directions.

Intensify the droop of your arms.
Bend your forearms at an angle
from your upper arms.

73

74

2. Pelvis and Moving

Cross your left leg diagonally over your right. Then step diagonally, forward and to the right, with your right foot. As you do this, raise your right hip.

Move backward: Cross your right leg backward diagonally toward the left, and step backward and to the side with your left leg. As you do it, lift your left hip toward the the left.

When you do this cross-step, bend your knees slightly, emphasizing the low-high movement with your body.

Add a sideways head movement, as in Pattern #1.

3. Double-time Movements of Your Pelvis

As you walk, do a hip lift with your free leg. Move your hip at twice the tempo of your step. For example: right, lift-left-hip twice. Step left, lift-right-hip twice.

Double-time your head movements in the same direction as your pelvic movement: short-short-long.

4. Movements of Your Arms

During the cross-step, circle your hands around each other, as if you're winding yarn. As you do the forward hip lift, swing your arms high and to the sides.

When you do the backward hip lift, stretch your arms back. Bend your upper body forward, if possible so that your back is horizontal to the floor.

5. Overall Coordination

When you do Exercises #1 through #4 diagonally, you are doing the disco step called "Tighten Up."

6. Variations: The Penguin

Do the step as a step-step-hop. Bend your knees slightly and hop flatly toward the sides. Right-left-hop right. Left-right-hop left.

At the same time, swing your pelvis toward the leg you're stepping with (not the one you're standing on). Lift your hip during the hop. As you lift your hip, keep your knee bent slightly and let your lower leg hang down loose, the sole of your foot parallel to the floor.

Tip your head toward your raised hip in rhythm with your feet. *Short-short-long.*

Your arms are stretched alongside your body with your hands angled outward (penguin-style).

The movement, which is very rapid, looks like the walk of a penguin. You can expand this basic form with other penguin figures and develop a penguin dance.

Soul Hip and Jingling

Practice Patterns for Pelvic Circles (illus. 74-79)

1. Pelvic Semi-circles and Direction of Movement

Shift your weight as you make each pelvic semi-circle forward.

Step toward the right with a pelvic semi-circle toward the right. Then step toward the left with a pelvic semi-circle toward the left.

Practice the same thing with pelvic semi-circles backward.

Practice the same thing with small steps forward and backward; when you do them, keep your feet parallel (not turned in or turned out).

Take 3 steps forward in each case, and on the fourth beat, lift your leg from your knee with a hip lift and clap your hands.

Do the same thing backward with clapping.

2. Pelvic Semi-circle and Head

Move your head in a semi-circle forward in the same tempo and in the same direction as your pelvic semi-circle.

When the pelvic movement is rapid, the circling of your head becomes a swinging of your head.

3. Your Arms are Fixed

Hold your hands on your hips or stretch them out in front of you, palms forward (illus. 75 and 76).

If you prefer, you can put 1 hand on your hip and extend the other (illus. 74). Change arms on the 4th beat, after you clap.

4. Overall Coordination

Patterns #1 through #3 produce the disco step called Jingling.

5. Full Pelvic Circles and More Coordinations

Make full circles with your head as you stand in a straddle position. Your head and your pelvis move together, forward and to the side, backward and to the side (illus. 78 and 79).

You can try the same thing with quarter, half and full turns in place (spiral movements).

Combine pelvic circles with low and high walking at the end of the exercise, in place.

The Latin Hip, the Skate, and the Cuban Walk

Practice Patterns for Backward Pelvic Movements (illus. 80)

These hip movements are found in Latin American dances, such as the samba and the rumba.

1. Latin Hip

Place your feet in a sideways straddle position. Bend your upper body forward slightly. When you step, place your weight on your right leg. Your hip will be leading backward toward the left.

2. Latin Hip and Head

That was the Latin Hip. Accompany it by swinging your head forward in half circles in the same direction as your hip, but in the opposite direction from the step.

3. Latin Hip and Shoulders

Make semi-circles back and forward in turns with your shoulders.

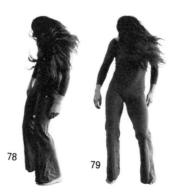

4. Latin Hip and Arms

Hold your arms out from your shoulders in opposite directions – your right shoulder projecting forward with your right arm extended backward, your left shoulder drawn back, with your left arm angled up from the elbow.

5. Overall Coordination

Combinations of Patterns #1 through #4 make up the disco figure, the "Skate", which you can vary by stepping sideways, clapping, and changing the arm movements.

6. Cuban Walk

Do Latin Hip in a semi-circle. Starting from the last position of shoulders and arms, as you take 1 step forward (weight on your right leg), you describe a semi-circle to the rear with your left hip. Then step to the left, moving your hip forward.

Practice Patterns for Contraction-Release

These coordinations lead to extreme movements of your back, from total rounding to full extension. The impulse can start between your shoulder blades, in your chest, or in your pelvis. It continues through your entire back, all the way, frequently, to your neck and head. It is a contraction (becoming small, pulling together) and release (letting loose, expanding), and it has been taken from American modern dance. You can alternate these movements impulsively, or do them gradually.

The movements are especially effective if you breathe with them: You inhale on the chest-expanding release (illus. 81), and exhale on the contraction (illus. 82) as you narrow your chest.

It's important to start the movement with a strong impulse. Begin it by consciously tensing your stomach muscles.

Position Exercises

1. Tailor's Position, holding your knees (see illus. 84-89)

Release: Draw up your knees, inhale, and stretch upward. Contraction: Draw back, starting

from your pelvis through the center of your chest, with your head sinking backward.

Try it with your head sinking forward.

2. From the same position, do it again, but this time exaggerate the backward-forward movements, bringing your chest so far forward that it's flat over the floor at the time of release.

Variation: Stretch your arms forward horizontally, and then move them to the side or the back.

3. Do the same movement sitting on your heels.

4. Sitting Sideways (hurdle position)

Sit on the floor, bending 1 leg at the knee in front of you. The other leg should be out to the side, and bent back at the knee. For convenience we'll call this the hurdle position, since it's close to the position that runners take when they jump over obstacles (illus. 81).

Support yourself with your left hand. Move back and forth diagonally as you do the contraction and release (illus. 82). Include your right arm in the movement. Keep it at shoulder height, moving it back and forth horizontally.

83

84

85

86

87

88

89

5. In Straddle Position

Lift your right ankle and turn your knee inward. With your upper body, contract as you make a quarter turn to the left.

As you do this, place your right hand on your left shoulder and reach forward with your left arm (illus. 91).

Release by turning your upper body back and returning your knee to its original position.

Do it the opposite way, starting with your left ankle.

6. In Space

Combine the contraction with 2 steps backward and the release with 2 steps forward, each with a partial knee bend.

Include your arms by making flowing horizontal circles at the same time (illus. 90).

Variation: Emphasize the forward movement by taking 2 steps forward, and 1 backward with a hesitation.
Count: Step-step-back-hold.

Emphasize the backward movement by doing the same thing to the back: step-step-forward-hold.

7. On the balls of your feet, with ankles and feet crossed, make a full pivot while you contract. End the movement with your opposite foot crossed over in front, in release position – feet flat, body lifted (illus. 92-94).

8. From Walking Forward

Cross your right leg over your left and start a complete turn to the left. Hold your arms forward, hands clasped, with your upper body in contraction.

Move a few steps backward in this position.

Start a full turn to the right (contracted), move a few steps backward in this position, bend your knees, and lower your body, continuing the turn until you arrive on the floor in a deeply bent position.

9. Standing, explore additional movements – walks, runs, hops, skips, jumps – in space, combining contraction and release.

10. Choreograph a mini-jazz dance, using various forms of contraction.

90

91

92

93

94

95

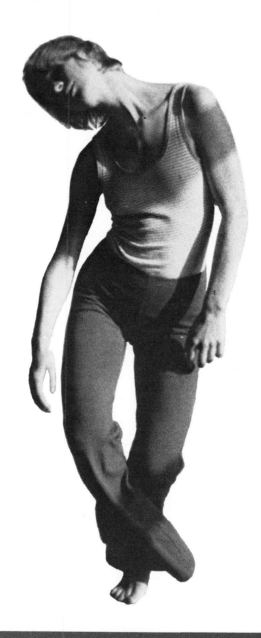

4 Contraction — Release in Jazz Dance

Relaxation, Flexion, Release

Contraction-Release in Jazz Dance

Relaxation, Flexion, Release

The Concept

Concepts such as relaxation, flexion and release can be summed up under the movement principle of contraction-release.

Relaxation

This means loosening your muscles or even letting them go slack and loose. In jazz dance, however, relaxation does not mean total release, but only partial relaxation of individual centers.

Release

This basic position in jazz dance means bending together, bending your upper body, hips and knees.

Flexion

This concept contrasts bending with stretching. Examples of flexion are the bending of your foot at an angle to your lower leg, your hand at an angle to your forearm, your forearm at an angle to your upper arm, or your chest at an angle to the bottom of your body. These are typical jazz positions.

Putting It Together

All these movements are based on contraction and release. Whether they are sudden or gradual, partial or complete, they all develop finely-tuned muscle sensations and they're important in creating artistic, expressive dances.

The sudden alternation of contraction and relaxation is especially important in jazz dance. Starting from total body contraction and relaxation in the following exercises, you'll gradually proceed to more intricate contraction-release patterns. The exercises are easier to do lying on the floor than sitting, kneeling or standing.

Be sure to use music as you work on this. It makes it easier and more stimulating. Start with music in which the dynamics change at fairly long intervals (contract for 4 beats, relax for 4 beats). Later, choose music with a shorter interval (2 beats and 1 beat).

Start out by lying on your back, on your stomach, or on your side.

Later use different sitting positions, stretching out your legs in front of you, sitting on your heels, in hurdle position (sitting sideways).

Then move on to standing positions: kneeling, deeply bent, half-bending, erect with crossed feet.

Body Exercises for Contraction and Release

1. Lying Down

Stretched out on your back (or your side, or your stomach), contract and relax your body in 4 counts. Then do it in 2 counts.

97

98

Contract with your arms held high, and then relax in a slightly rounded position.

Contract in a curled-up position. Relax in the open position.

Starting from any floor position with relaxed muscles, change into any different position while contracting your entire body. Do this gradually at first, then suddenly. Change back as you relax.

2. Sitting

Practice contraction and relaxation of all your muscles in a variety of sitting positions. Emphasize the contraction by rapidly stretching or lifting your arms to the side (illus. 98), to the back or up high.

3. Kneeling

Contract your muscles starting from a variety of kneeling positions. Combine them with straightening up and stretching. Use your arms, emphasizing forward and upward movements. Make the release sudden. Accent it by sinking into a resting position, or going back to your original position.

Start by sitting on your heels with knees open or closed. Contract as you straighten up into a kneeling position. Reach high, sideways or backward with extended arms (illus. 101).

Start relaxed, sitting sideways with your leg placed forward, to the side or to the rear. Straighten up suddenly into a knee-walk position. Your upper body should be bent

slightly – forward, back or to the side – and with highly emphasized extended arms. Return to your original position.

Sitting with your hips on your heels, back rounded, and arms by your sides, push yourself away from the floor with your hands and straighten up fully. Then return to your initial position.

Start sitting on your heels with your upper body relaxed, forehead on the floor (illus. 100). Lift into a contracted kneeling position, with your back parallel to the floor, your arms stretched in the forward or rear position (illus. 101).

Start relaxed, sitting with your upper thighs to the right or left. Suddenly, contract your body. Use 1 hand to support you as you lift

99

100

101

yourself into a sideways bridge. Your free arm should stretch sideways or up.

Explore more variations starting from these positions.

4. Standing

Start from a variety of positions: deeply bent, stretched, walking, standing on the balls of your feet or on 1 leg. Contract all your muscles with various arm extensions, and then suddenly relax your arms, head, body and legs.

After this, relax, shake, loosen up. Fall down into a deeply bent straddle position.

Standing, with your body and arms hanging down loosely, raise your upper body so that it's horizontal to the floor. Extend your arms forward or backward.

5. Transitions from One Position to Another

Change from a position on your stomach, back or side into some type of sitting and fall back again.

Then change from a floor position into a sitting position, into a kneeling position and finally an erect position.

Do the opposite. From an erect position, relax into a kneel, a sit, and a position on the floor – 1 after the other.

6. Loosening Up for Jumping

Make a stretchy jump (illus. 105).

Immediately after you land, let yourself fall into a deeply bent position (illus. 104) or sit on your heels and roll into a position on the floor.

Jump into a straddle, wide straddle, or deeply bent position, and then roll onto the floor.

Practice this to a count of 4, increasing the tempo until you are doing the entire sequence in 1 beat.

Contraction and Release Exercises for Individual Parts of the Body

Exercises for Your Hands and Arms

You'll be using your arms and hands as a means of expression

102

103

104

105

106

in jazz dance more than in other types of dance, so you need to give them a good deal of attention.

1. Lift 1 arm or both arms as if holding off an imaginary force (illus. 102). Do it slowly or rapidly from a low position into sideways, forward, backward or erect positions. Then let them drop.

2. Bending halfway over (illus. 106), stretch your arms rapidly and forcefully in various directions. Spread your fingers and draw your arms back to your body again.

3. Swing both arms together in 1 direction and then change to the opposite direction, as you bend and stretch your elbows (see Swinging, Chapter 5).

4. Connect the arm movements above with various types of movement: walking, running, hopping, jumping, turning, falling, and twisting. You can get more ideas if you look at the arm movements on pages 50 and 51.

Exercises for Your Legs and Feet

1. Bend and stretch your knee slightly with the emphasis on the stretch. Alternate slow and fast movements and vibrating movements. Accentuate the rhythm by snapping your fingers.

2. Do the same thing standing with your weight on 1 leg and the other leg off to 1 side. Shift your weight to the other leg after the first, second or third beat.

3. Bend your body, round your back, your hands supporting you on the floor. After twisting your body 2 to 4 times, put your weight on the balls of your feet and straighten your knees. Let your hands stay on the floor. Then fall back into your original rounded position.

4. Jump into a standing position on the balls of your feet. Hold yourself there briefly, and then allow yourself to fall into a slightly bent-knee position, your head sinking onto your chest.

107

Do the same thing on 1 leg with the other leg bent slightly forward or to the side.

5. Now look at illus. 107. Assume a wide straddle position. Keep your weight (and your pelvis) low between your legs. Your upper body should be erect, your arms stretched out in front of you.

Dip deeply 3 counts, and extend your leg on the fourth.

Do the same thing while you shift your weight from the center to the right and to the left.

Do the same thing extending your arms 1 at a time. With your right hand, grasp for your left toes. Extend your left arm upward and to the left.

Your weight is located deep to the left; your right leg is extended. Do it to the other side after the third, second or first beat. Extend your leg at different intervals. First count 1-2 and extend your leg to the other side on 3 and hold 4.

Next time, count 1 – extend to the other side on 2 – and hold 3 and 4.

Then next time, extend to the opposite side on 1 and hold 2, 3 and 4.

6. Try long, stretched jumps from 3 different positions: first from a rounded back position, knees bent; then from a deeper bent-knee straddle, and then from a walk.

Do the same thing with quarter, half, and full turns during the jump. Finish in a relaxed, rounded position with knees bent.

You'll find more ideas for jumps in the next chapter.

Exercises for Your Upper Body

1. Lie on your back with your arms at your sides. Contract and lift your chest from the floor, while your shoulders, pelvis, and legs remain relaxed. Draw yourself up into a tall sitting position. Lie down again, but on the way back, roll down vertebra by vertebra, or stretch your back as you lie down.

2. Loosen your upper body and your arms by dipping forward (relaxed) as you sit on the floor with your legs stretched out in front of you or in the hurdle position. Then straighten up, lifting yourself sideways and supporting your

body with 1 hand. Shift to your knees, kneel, and let your upper body fall forward loosely. Then circle, with your upper body, to the side, and back. To finish, straighten up rapidly, pulling your shoulders back and down.

Do the same thing, but this time, at the finish, stretch and raise your body. (See illus. 108.)

With a partner

3. Loosen and then stretch your body while you walk together or toward each other.

4. Start from a rounded, deeply bent straddle, one hand behind your body, supporting you, the

other angled upward, palm toward the ceiling. Move into a standing position by pushing your pelvis – and then the rest of your body – up and forward in a large body wave (illus. 109-111).

5. In the same starting position, but a little lower, stretch your arms out in front of you, clasp your hands, and dip forward deeply, swinging your head and arms through your legs.

6. In the same starting position, hold your ankles from behind. Lift your head, straighten your back, so it is horizontal to the floor, and keep your buttocks as low as possible. Hold this position for 2, 4 or 8 beats.

108

109

110

111

7. Do these exercises, 1 after the other. The important thing is the spontaneous switching back and forth of contraction and release in a rhythmic, dynamic way. Music will help!

Tension and Relaxation Exercises

What is tension? It is control of your body – the moments when your body is ready to move – alert, stretched. It isn't muscular tension. In order to use tension properly, your body must be relaxed, but ready.

Relaxation is a loosening of all the body pressures, so that there is no stress anywhere in any part of your body. It isn't falling apart carelessly. It still, though loose and free, has a consciousness of the center of the body.

For Tension in Movement

1. Stand on 1 leg (it can be bent or straight). Move your free leg slowly or rapidly in various directions and at different levels, forward, to the sides, to the back.

2. Bend your free leg at the knee, angle your foot down, and move it, in this position, in various directions and levels. Move it flat on the floor or bent and high.

Your upper body can be lifted, straight or rounded. It can lean forward, sideways, or to the rear.

112   113

114   115

3. After you stand on 1 leg for a relatively long time – 4, 8, or 16 beats – switch legs. Let the music determine when. Include your arms in the overall movement. Stretch them, spread your fingers or close them in a fist.

These exercises (illus. 112-118) train your feeling for balance as well as tension. They also fit into creative dances wonderfully well.

For Relaxation in Movement

1. You do this exercise with a partner. Close your eyes, loosen up your body, and end in a bent position, knees bent slightly, head and arms hanging down loosely.

Your partner gently prods your arms and shoulders, your chest, your hips, or your head. Give in

to these impulses loosely and softly. Move – quietly – in whatever way your body feels like moving.

2. In the same relaxed condition, give yourself inner impulses by starting the movements with your head, from 1 shoulder, from your chest or your pelvis, and follow the movement loosely and tumblingly. Keep only enough tension in your body so that you don't fall down.

3. From a standing position, *fall* into a relaxed, rounded, deeply-bent position. Let your head fall back first, then forward. Let your hands support you on the floor. Slowly straighten your knees. Then straighten up with your upper body (illus. 119-121).

Alternate this falling and standing in a flowing way.

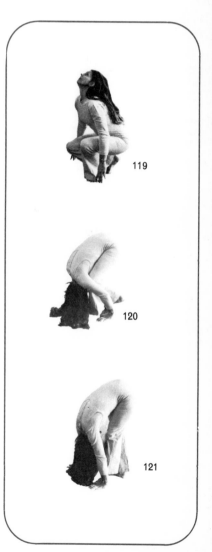

119

120

121

116

117

118

55

5 Jazz Movements
Based on Simple Gymnastics

Walking, Running, Hopping, Jumping
Swinging, Turning & Combinations of Steps

Jazz Movements Based on Simple Gymnastics

Walking, Running, Hopping, Jumping, Swinging, Turning and Combinations of Steps

There are 2 basic types of movement in jazz dance: motion and locomotion.

Motion is the inner body movement you do more or less in 1 spot. Locomotion means that you move through space in various paths and directions – forward, backward, sideways or diagonally.

Walking, running, hopping, jumping and turning are present in all the dances of the world. Springing and swinging are present in every movement, visibly or in a less pronounced way. Springing is an elastic yielding of all your joints (particularly your hips and knees and ankles) as you move upward. Swinging is done in pendulum-like, circling, or guided movements of your arms, legs, body and head. In jazz these

movements are very different from those of traditional gymnastics. They lead a life of their own in jazz dance. They give character to a movement. They are part of "motion" – inner body movements you do in 1 spot.

Everyday movements are the basis of jazz dance. They aren't limited by the jazz technique and style, but enlarged and made much more interesting and unpredictable. A whole world of new possibilities of movement opens up when you put together what you've already learned with simple walks, runs and jumps.

Jazz Walks

Jazz walks often call for double-time foot movements, the transfer of your weight from 1 leg to the

other, subdivided into 2 or more movements. Here are a few simple 2-element walking forms for you to try:

1. Flat Jazz Walk

Place your right foot on the floor with no weight on it at first. On the second beat, step on it, bend your right knee, and lift your left leg from the floor (illus. 123). The count goes 1-AND, 2-AND, and so on.

2. Ball Drop Jazz Walk

Place your heel on the floor with your knee bent. On the second beat, put your whole foot down. Swing your arms in an accented way, with your elbows out at an angle opposite to that of your feet (illus. 124 and 125).

123

124

125

126

127

128

3. Heel Drop Jazz Walk

Place the ball of your foot on the floor. On the second beat, put your whole foot down with an accent on the heel. As you do it, hold your forearms horizontally in front of your body. Swing them up and down together loosely while you snap your fingers (illus. 126).

As a rule, jazz walks are guided from isolated hip movements. Other centers, such as your head, shoulders, arms and chest, are coordinated with the hip movements. Some of these coordinations occur frequently, are definite "steps," and have special names. Here are a few of them:

4. Jazz Walk with Hip Lift

With hip lift, walk forward, backward, or sideways with cross-steps.

5. Reggae Walk

This is a jazz walk with Soul Hip. Make semi-circular movements with your hips while your leg falls loosely from your bent knee (illus. 127).

6. Cuban Walk

This is a jazz walk with Latin Hip (illus. 130). In this walk, your hip is behind your step. For example, when walking left, your chest leads diagonally forward, while your hips move backward and to the right. Make appropriate head and arm movements to the side or in a semi-circle.

129

130

7. Funky Walk

With slightly bent knees, walk on the balls of your feet, swinging your pelvis back and forth. Make appropriate head and arm movements forward and backward (illus. 131-138).

8. Boogie Walk

Hips swing to the right and left, forward and sideways (illus. 139).

You can vary your arm, head, and shoulder movements and add accents by clapping, finger snapping, stamping and in many other ways. Be sure to emphasize the syncopation which is essential to the jazz walk – putting the accent on a normally weak beat. A syncopated count would go: One TWO three FOUR.

131   132   133   134

135   136   137   138

139

9. Chicken Walk

Stand on the balls of your feet. Turn your bent knee in and out. When you lift your right leg, turn your knees toward each other. When your weight is on your right leg, turn your legs away from each other. Do the same thing walking to the left (illus. 140-142).

10. African Walk (in triple-time)

Place your right foot forward, flat, and without putting your weight on it. Rapidly lift your right knee into a horizontal stretched position. Lower your right leg, place it on the floor, and put your weight on it. Do the same thing with your left leg.

When you lift your knee, your upper body moves along with it, and your head falls slightly toward your back. Let your arms hang loosely, or extend them alongside your body, hands turned out (illus. 143).

Variation: You can expand this walk into quadruple-time. Start by raising your knee, then lift it up twice even more rapidly before the next transfer of your weight.

140   141   142

143

Jazz Runs

The typical jazz run is a low jumping run which has a moment of flying in every step. You can vary it and make it more complex by adding motions (inner body movements).

1. Lift your right knee high in front and then, as you come down, drop your right leg back further than usual. Swing your left leg high in back, starting from your knee (illus. 144). Continue the run.

2. Let the movement run through your back. Your upper body should have a soft, flowing, slightly snaky movement.

3. As you perform this jumping run, work your other centers in strong opposing movements. Or pull your arms toward your body as you make sideways movements with your head.

4. Do an isolation movement with your head as you run, in a forward-backward or right-left movement.

5. Do a jazz run lifting your lower leg forward and to the side (a kind of shambling run).

6. Do the same thing running backward. Swing your lower leg backward in a semi-circle. Draw your knees back as far as possible when you do this.

Practice the jumping run so that you can move your free leg forward, to the side, or in a semi-circle flat above the floor. Then expand the movement in each case with just one of these coordinations. Later you can bring several centers into play to give your jazz run a different character. Use your head, body, and arms in any way that feels right.

Jazz Hops

Hopping is a natural way to move, and it's frequently used in folk dancing. This is a typical hop from African dance:

1. Do a hop-walk, knees bent, upper body bent forward.

As you do it, lift your arms to the side with your forearms bent down. You can accent the movement by dipping your elbows up and down forcefully.

144

2. Vary the hopping with different tempos:

Stamping – earthbound hopping
Flat – gliding hopping
Flying – light hopping

3. Accentuate the hop by lifting your knees sharply and then placing your feet down lightly without a sound.

Reverse directions while you hop.

4. Hopping in double-time: Give a flat hop to the left, placing your right foot down without any weight on it. Then immediately lift your right leg emphatically from your knee.

You can repeat this knee movement 2 or 3 times and with 2 or 3 hops to the left. In each case, your upper body should move toward the leg you have raised.

Extend your arms alongside your body, hands turned outward. Every time you raise your knee, push your hands down to the level of your raised foot.

5. Do many hops on 1 leg to the side. Bend or stretch your other leg to the side while giving a swing to the hop. It becomes a skip (illus. 146).

6. Try this combination: 4 jazz run steps forward, 4 hops to the right, 4 jazz run steps forward, 4 hops to the left, like this:

145

146

147

148

149

Do a hop in place to finish the combination (illus. 150 and 151) with loose movements of your head, shoulders, arms and body, bending forward, sideways and backward. Use hip movements as well.

7. Hip combination: Perform 1 of these hops, bending or stretching your free leg to the side at the same time.

Combine the same thing with a half turn for each hop. As you hop, bend your free leg backward slightly at the knee and stretch it far to the rear. As you do it, stretch 1 or both arms out sideways (illus. 152).

Turn your head toward the rear, glancing over your shoulder toward the bottom of the foot of your lifted leg, stretching your upper body backward (illus. 153).

Intensify this into a jump.

Jazz Jumps

Usually, in a jazz jump, your legs are not extended, but bent at the hips, knees, or ankles. Your arms are frequently drawn in, so that the jump gives the impression that your body is bent, contracted, that you are earthbound – the opposite of jumps in ballet which seem free from gravity (illus. 154).

Of course, jazz also has jumps that seem free from gravity, but you do them in a similar way to regular ballet jumps.

Here are 4 basic jazz jumps:

1. Two-leg jumps
Jump and land with both legs simultaneously, finishing in a rounded bent position or a straddle.

2. One-leg jumps
Jump and land on the same leg.

3. Alternating jumps
Jump from 1 leg and land on the other. (Most gymnastic and dance jumps belong to this type, such as running, horse, turning and scissor jumps.)

4. Combination jumps
Jump off both legs, land on 1 leg. Or jump off 1 leg and land on both.

154

Experiment with these jumps. There are many kinds you can do from gymnastics, acrobatics, and athletics, as well as other styles of dance. Apart from their height and width, they differ in what you do when you're up in the air. The possibilities for "fantasy" jumps are just about unlimited. Try some of the following ideas, and then add more of your own.

In the Air

Rounded, deeply bent jump
1. Jump off and land with both feet. During the jump, raise your knee (closed or open) toward your chest. Bend your upper body, your shoulders. Move your head forward. Try out different positions to go with it (illus. **155-158**).

2. Do the same jump with closed knees. In the air, move both knees rapidly toward the right, left and to the right again.

3. Do the same jump as in #2, but this time give it a quarter, half, three-quarter or full turn (illus. **162**).

4. During the jump, cross your arms and legs in front of your body (illus. **159**).

5. During the jump, bend your body to the side and move your arms in the opposite direction (illus. **161**).

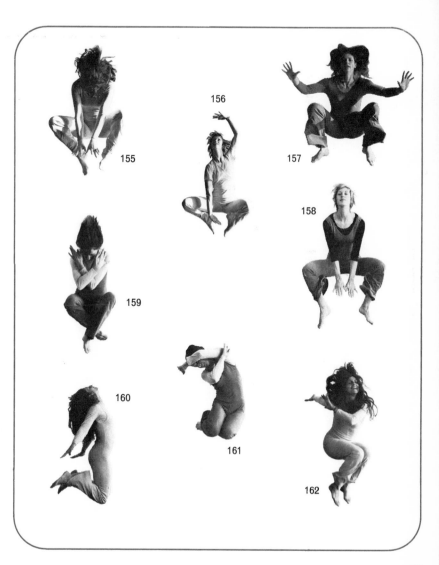

155

156

157

158

159

160

161

162

Horse jumps
1. Jump from 1 leg. In the air, lift your knees forward, 1 after the other, up to a horizontal position. Bend your upper body and head forward, and draw your arms in front of your chest (illus. 154).

2. Cross your feet. Jump and land with them crossed, but in the other direction (illus. 159).

Walking or running jumps
1. Jump off your right leg, land on your left leg. While you're in the air, lift your left leg, knee high, foot pointing down. Twist your body toward your left leg. Stretch your arms down and to the side, angle your hands up (illus. 164).

Try other arm positions.

2. Turn your chest forward as you jump or to the right side (away from the swinging leg). Make other movements in the air with your arms, hands, head, legs, and feet.

3. Start the jump with your knees bent. Swing your lower leg forward and the other backward. Push your hands away from your body to the sides, holding your palms out (illus. 166).

Put together a sequence of jazzy running jumps, after you master each basic form.

Turning jumps
1. In a rounded position, low, with knees bent, start the jump with both legs, or jump off 1 leg and land on both (illus. 170).

2. Start a 2-leg jump from a low sideways straddle position. During the jump, do half or full turns. Hold your arms up, or down to the side (illus. 171).

3. Do turning jumps from runs or sideways walks, turning forward or backward. Jump in straight lines or curves with different arm, leg and body movements (illus. 165 and 166).

The charm of jazz fantasy jumps is that only the start and landing are fixed. When you're in the air, you discover for yourself the shape of the jump!

Cross jump
This delightful jump (illus. 167-168) is quick to learn.

From a diagonal run of 3 steps (right, left, right), start the jump from your right leg. Swing your left leg over your right leg to meet it. Land on your left leg.

When you're in the air, bend your left leg slightly at the knee. Angle your right leg sharply at the knee, bringing it flat under your body (almost horizontal to the floor).

You can move your arms up or put them in a jazz position with your elbows close to your body, moving your forearms horizontally to the sides (illus. 174).
Spread your fingers and turn your palms forward. Move your head in the direction opposite the jump.

Side jump
Cross your right leg behind your left leg. Step sideways with your left leg. Now cross your right leg in front of your left leg and start the jump, bringing your left leg up to the left in a bent position with your foot drawn close (illus. 172).

While you're in the air, turn your hips and upper body sharply from left to right – away from the direction of the jump (illus. 173).

Come down on your left leg. As you come down, immediately cross your right leg behind your left leg, ending up with your weight on your right leg. Now you are ready to start again with the other leg.

Experiment with other fantasy jumps.

172

173

174

175

176

177

Jazz Turns

You can do turns in place or moving through space. In the first case, turns are "motions," and in the second, locomotion. Borrowed from gymnastics, folk dance and classical ballet, turns and pirouettes are found in many jazz compositions, but in jazz, we change them a little.

There are 3 basic turns:
  turning on both legs (step turns)
  turning on 1 leg (pirouettes)
  turning in the air (turning jumps)

Step turns

This is the simplest form of turning. You can do low, middle, or high turns with several short or longer steps, either in place or while moving (spiral turns).

You can accompany step turns with isolation movements of the pelvis, shoulders, head, arms and hands. Often, step turns are done with the body in the release position, with emphatic up and down arm movements.

Experiment freely to develop interesting step turns.

1. Three-step Turn

Do a full turn, a half turn or 1½ turns within 3 steps. Finish with a hop on the fourth beat.

Bend your knees on the first step; go up on the balls of your feet, straightening your legs on the second step; bend your knees again on the third beat. Emphasize the low-high-low-hop movement. Accent it (illus. 178 and 179).

2. Crossed Turn (illus. 181-183)

This turn has 3 parts. In the first part, make a full turn to the right, crossing your left leg over your right. For the second part, make a half turn to the right, ending up with your legs slightly open and parallel. For the third part, make another half turn to the right. At the end of that turn, your right leg will be crossed over your left. Be sure to keep the parts distinctly separate.

Combine this turn with low-high-low movements.

Arm movements: In the low position, draw your arms close to your body. In the high position, extend your arms rapidly up and out. In the low position, draw them back to your body.

178   179

180

181

182   183

Include your head and body in the movement by bending, raising, and bending them again rapidly at chest level.

3. Contraction Turn (illus. 184-187)

With your feet crossed, and up on the balls of your feet, turn smoothly as you do a contraction with bent knees or standing erect.

You can include your arms in different ways. For example, bend your arms close to your body, palms facing out. Or extend your arms forward at shoulder level, and place your head between them as you turn (illus. 185). You can also clasp your hands as you do this (illus. 186).

Jazz pirouettes (1-leg turns)

One leg movements come from ballet. You do them on the balls of your feet, with a drawn-out movement of your arms, your upper body, or your free leg. It is important to have a feeling for the vertical line of your body, for your control and balance.

1. Turn on 1 leg: Do a full turn, 1½ turns, or a double turn, forward or backward. End the turn in a straddle position with bent knees.

2. Do a 1-leg turn with the free leg bent. This time, as you turn, bend your free leg forward or lift it to the side or back.

Stretch or contract your body. Bend your standing leg at the knee. Bring your arms and your head into the contraction.

3. Try it with your free leg extended sideways, forward, backward, or crossing over your standing leg

Bend or stretch your standing leg. Also stretch your body or bend it backward (illus. 188).

Stretch your arms out wide to the side, back, or up high.

4. Do the 1-leg turn on the balls of your feet, with both legs extended, at first. Contract your body (round your back at chest level) and lift 1 knee forward and up into a horizontal position.

Spread your fingers in front of your face (illus. 177).

5. Combine pirouettes with running steps.

184

185 186 187

188

6. Do turns with your partner, harmonizing your turn to his or hers.

7. Find a sequence which you want to repeat, and develop a jazz composition around it.

Springing in Jazz Gymnastics

Springing is a vertical movement, which you do mostly in place.

Movement Patterns

1. Spring with both legs. Without ever leaving the floor, stand first on your whole foot and then spring onto the balls of your feet.

Do it with 1 foot and then the other.

Combine this springing with arm, chest and head positions that you've learned.

2. Do deep bending ankle springs ending with straight knees. Shift your weight after springing once, twice, or several times, from 1 leg to the other.

3. Spring lightly, shifting your weight forward or backward, and then to the right and left as you stand in straddle position.

Move your pelvis with your body. Then move it in the opposite direction.

Do it while you twist your body in the opposite direction.

4. Coordinate movements of other centers. For example, trace easy forward and backward circles with your arms. Then add your head and hips. On the fourth beat, do the spring once, slowly circling your arms.

5. Accent your foot springs by stamping with your heels. Try it with 1 leg or both.

Bend deeply as you stamp. Add movements of other centers, especially hands and arms.

Invent other combinations.

6. Knee springs
Bend your knees slightly and then spring up, extending them.

Do it moving forward, sideways and backward with the soles of your feet flat.

Contract as you step.

Try it with a rapid extension of your leg.

7. Hip springs
With your legs stretched, do a springing dip of your upper body with your back straight. This movement can be small or large. With each step you take, dip your body diagonally, horizontally, or forward, deeply.

8. Arm springs
Start with your arms at your sides.

189

190

Bend your elbows slightly, and then forcefully spring them up and down. Keep your hands at 1 level in front of you, fingertips touching, while your elbows move (illus. 184).

Try this arm spring with a jazz hop.

9. Head springs
Dip your head slightly up and down by lifting and lowering your chin.

Combine head and knee springs. Bend your head forward when you bend your knees. When you straighten your knees, dip your head back.

Try it the other way, bending your head backward as you bend your knees and forward when you straighten them.

10. All-over spring
Relax every part of your body. Now spring in your ankles, knees and hips with your body bent forward deeply.

Allow the movements to pass through your body from your feet to your head.

Include a strong arm spring forward.

Your entire body is involved in this intense spring (see photo on page 75).

191

Swinging

This basic gymnastic and dance form is found in every movement in some way. There are several types of swings, and they vary depending on their direction and the part of your body that does them. There are pendulum swings and circle swings; beating, pushing, whipping, lifting and drawing movements are all swings used in in jazz dance.

You can do them in front of your body, alongside it, at various levels, diagonally, or in combination, such as circular swings and figure 8's.

It's easy to swing your arms, legs and your whole body. If you work on isolating them, you can swing smaller areas, too, such as your head, forearms, lower legs and pelvis.

Your Arms in Jazz Dance

In jazz dance, your arm moves starting from your shoulders.

192

Its line is often broken up into parts – upper arm, forearm, fingers. Each part is important and by changing its position and direction, you can change the character of a movement completely.

Hand Patterns

1. Standing in a straddle position, stretch your arms out to the sides. Open your hands alternately, spread your fingers and then close them into fists.

Combine these movements with the slow lifting of your arms upward and back.

Do it rhythmically and combine it with steps, jazz walks and turns.

2. Arms relaxed, shake out your hands loosely. Then – 1 arm at a time – starting from your elbows, bend and stretch your arms in each direction swinging your hands away loosely at the wrist (illus. 192).

3. Circle your hands inward and outward 1 at a time, while you stretch out your arms in each direction.

Do it in rhythm with running steps.

4. Shake and circle your hands, holding your arms in different positions.

193

Do it while you walk in a straight line and on small curved lines.

Enlarge the movement by shaking your upper arms and forearms along with your hands.

5. Circle your hands around each other, as if you're winding yarn.

Do it with your forearms.

Arm Patterns

1. Extend your arms alongside your body. Angle your hands in or out in various directions.

2. Extend your arms at shoulder height, palms facing out. Spread your fingers (illus. 198).

3. With arms extended alongside your body, roll them in and out from your shoulders. Bend and round your back in and out, as you do it.

Do the same thing with an opposing movement – twisting your shoulders.

4. Extend your arms diagonally to the sides above your head. Spread your fingers, palms forward – facing each other or hanging down (illus. 194-197).

5. Bend your elbows and hold them horizontally, palms in front of your chest, hanging down toward your body or opened to the ceiling (illus. 199).

6. Extend your arms forward in front of your body, palms forward, fingers extended upward (illus. 198) or down (illus. 200).

Do the same thing with 1 arm. Keep the other arm tight against your body, palms spread on your hip (see illus. 202).

201   202

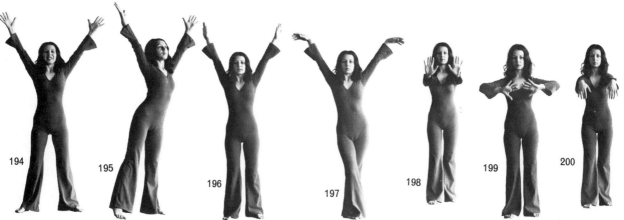

194   195   196   197   198   199   200

7. Hold both arms in a V position, hands at shoulder level. Draw your arms back as far as possible. Draw your shoulder blades together and lean backwards as you do this.

8. Extend your upper body forward almost horizontally, with your back straight. Stretch your arms diagonally backward. Angle your hands toward the outside (illus. 201) or extend them toward the floor.

9. Cross your forearms in front of your chest, hands spread in front of your face.

10. Look for new arm movements to accompany the jazz movements. Combine these arm movements with flowing transitions. You'll see a few more possibilities in the illustrations.

Experiment with free arm movement and different tempos with appropriate music.

Accent the start of the movement and then let it subside.

Start slowly, accelerate, put the accent at the end of your arm movement – then stop abruptly.

2. Arm directions
Hold your arms parallel and move them simultaneously in different directions.

Now hold them parallel, but move one after the other, covering the the same paths.

This time try moving your arms at the same time, but in opposition.

Or move them in opposing directions, 1 after the other.

Practice all the possibilities with music.

Work with a partner as a mirror image.

3. Arm positions
With your arm extended, guide it upward, leading with the edge of your hand (thumb side – then little finger side).

Indicate the direction of the movement with the inside or outside of your hands.

Guide the arm movement from your elbow. Move high and low, in circles and figure 8's and spirals.

Movement Patterns for Your Arms

Free arm movements are rare in Western dance. As a result, we're not used to doing them and they take practice.

1. Arm dynamics
You can do soft, flowing arm movements, stretched, angular arm movements, or explosive ones.

203 204

205 206

207

4. Arm impulses
Do the arm positions listed above with different rhythmic counts. Let the arm movement provide the impulse for other movements which will follow.

5. Arm accompaniments
You can develop arm movements to go with every jazz movement. Try to work out those that are strongest and most appropriate.

6. Arm swings
These are gymnastics swinging movements, but with syncopated jazz rhythms. Try these:

Spirals over your head

Front and side swings and circles, with both arms or with each arm in opposite directions (illus. 203)

Arm swings up high, with accented hopping

Figure 8 swings guided by your elbows (illus. 204)

Horizontal swings

Spiral swings, with 1 arm or both arms in front of your body and over your head, parallel to each other, 1 after the other, or in opposite directions (illus. 205-207).

Your Legs and Feet in Jazz Dance

Foot Movements

1. Standing – or sitting down – bend, extend and circle your feet slowly and rapidly to music.

2. Put your heel and the balls of your feet on the floor at the same time. Raise your arch and toes.

3. Place the tips of your toes and your heels on the floor and draw up your arch.

4. Roll your feet from the heels to the balls in 2 beats, first 1 foot at a time in place, and then while moving (see Jazz Walks, pages 58-61).

5. Stand first on the balls of your feet and then on your full foot as you go through sequences of tension and relaxation.

6. Practice a walk and run, rolling through your foot from ball to heel (see Jazz Walks, pages 58-61).

Leg Swings

1. Bend the leg you are standing on. Extend the other leg and put it out in various directions.

Do the same thing, turning your leg in and out from your hip.

2. Kicking

Leaving your foot loose, swing your lower leg, starting from your knee, forward, diagonally, and to the side.

3. Flings (throwing your leg)

Fling your leg out from your thigh and hip. Fling it high, forward and to the side (illus. 208).

At the same time, snap your fingers or clap and stretch your body forward (illus. 209).

4. Crossing

Cross 1 foot over the other, first closely, and then widely. Combine this with running steps, and turns.

5. Brushing

Wipe your foot flatly over the floor, forward and back, to the side, to the front or behind the leg you are standing on.

Do the same thing while you move in a kind of shuffle.

6. Tripping steps

Transfer your weight rapidly from foot to foot. Right-left-right and left-right-left.

7. Sliding

Slide on both legs or on 1 leg in various directions with the entire foot and your whole weight on the floor. The movement should start from your bent knees.

Step Combinations

1. Step-step-step-hop

Taking 3 steps – right-left-right-hop – hop flatly from the right foot and immediately catch yourself, knees bent, on your entire foot. Start the same sequence to the left.

You can hold your arms parallel to each other, high up, and diagonally to the right – or in other directions – behind you, for example.

When you raise your knee during the hop, you can lift it from the hip or turn it toward your standing leg and then toward the outside, turning in and out from your hip joint.

Make a quarter turn as you do the hop.

Taking running steps to the side, make a half or full turn with the hop, then a quarter or $\frac{3}{4}$ turn, and continue the step in a different direction.

Try this sequence with a partner, adjusting to each others' movement. Each time you hop, "recognize" your partner coming toward you, and hop toward each other.

2. Sideways Cross

Step sideways to the right. Cross your left foot forward over your right foot on the second step.

Now do the same thing toward the back.

Combine the two steps: First do them forward, then to the back.

To a 2-count: Emphasize and delay the sideways step, so the count

208

209

is *long-short*. Intensify the cross step by gently jumping out of it to start the next step.

Arm movements: Hold your right arm out toward the right. Move it up when you cross feet, then to the left, and down (making a circle toward the front of you). Do the same thing with both arms.

The entire sequence flows. Dance it with intensity or with reservation.

3. New Jersey (backward step sequence)

Pull your pelvis back and bend your upper body forward. Take a step to the left and backward, and as you do it, lean your body backward. It looks as if you're falling. At the same time, turn your right foot to the right on your heel, and take a step back and to the right. Then turn out your left foot to the left and continue stepping backward, flowing first to the right and then to the left.

Arm movements: As you turn your right foot out, lift your right forearm with bent elbow. Hang the back of your hand toward your shoulder. Your left arm should be up with bent elbow, too, but in a diagonal position (illus. 207). Swing your head in a semi-circle front, toward the turned-out leg.

The New Jersey is a loose, lazy movement.

Try this combination:
4 New Jersey steps back,
4 bent-knee steps forward in a zigzag path backward and forward or a figure 8.

Variation:
New Jersey step to the side then to the left
and step to the left side.
Turn your right toe out toward the right.
Step on your right heel.
Repeat the 2-beat movement several times to the left. Move to the right occasionally.

Arm movements: When you bend your body forward, extend your arms in front of your body, hands clasped (illus. 210).

210   211

Swing both hands to the left over your shoulder (elbows bent) and bring them back down to the right beside your thigh (elbows straight). This is a diagonal swing in front of you, from the upper left (when your right leg is turned out; see illus. 211) toward the lower right in the bent position (illus. 210).

4. Jazz Waltz

Take any simple step pattern in 3/4 rhythm. Try emphasizing different beats rapidly and smoothly, starting with the first beat, then going on to the second alone, and then the third alone.

Arm movements: Hold your arms to the side, slightly below shoulder level. Push your shoulders forward in turns, in reverse of what your legs are doing. Do the shoulder movement only on the first beat.

Try different arm swings. You can use circular swings, moving both arms at the same time. Or use only 1 arm moving in the direction you're going (or in the opposite direction).

Try horizontal circle swings (like breast-stroke swimming movements) with the 3/4 rhythm. Let your head and back move along with your arms.

Start with large, soft movements, expand them, and then gradually make them much smaller.

212

213

6 Natural Movement Forms & Techniques in Jazz Dance

Natural Movement Forms & Techniques in Jazz Dance

Opposing Movements

If you intensify the movements you make naturally, you automatically get "opposing" movements. Take walking, for example. As your right foot moves forward, so does your left hand. This is an "opposing" movement.

You make opposing movements as you turn portions of your body toward each other: your head, shoulders, arms, torso, pelvis, and legs. Then you can combine them with bending, extending, stretching and turning movements. This makes for an enormous number of variations which create new forms and means of expression.

Twisting

Twisting movements require stretching and coordination. But they come naturally, so they're simple movements to make. You'll discover many possibilities as you do the following exercises and they are easy to incorporate into your dancing. Do them with music.

You can twist in many ways:
Turn your pelvis in opposition to your feet.
Turn your upper body in opposition to your legs or feet.

Turn one shoulder in opposition to the other shoulder.
Twist your shoulders in relation to your pelvis.

You can't distinguish sharply between opposing movements and twisting. They are frequently the same thing. You can intensify an opposing movement by twisting.

Lying Down

Do opposing movements while lying on your back or stomach. For example:

1. Move your legs and pelvis opposite to your shoulders. Develop this movement further so that you're rolling and twisting on the floor.

Combine the twisting with levels, so that you writhe gradually into a standing position.

2. Lying on your back, move your right knee toward your left shoulder. Then move your left knee toward your right shoulder.

3. Lying on your back with your arms to your sides, raise your right leg and extend it toward your left hand.

4. Lying on your back, turn both feet (tight together) toward the left.

Then turn your pelvis, body and shoulders toward the left, too. Turn your body onto your side as a result of this twisting.

5. On your stomach, with your forearms over your head, move your right leg (bent at the knee) backward over your left leg. Reverse the sequence with the other leg. Only lift 1 hip off the floor each time.

Continue this movement, turning onto your side, with 1 hand on the floor. Keep your straight leg down with its heel on the floor. Your pelvis is lifted up. From this position stand up, with a large wave through your body, for example.

Sitting

1. While sitting on the floor, hands behind you supporting you, knees up and bent, bend and turn your shoulders and arms to the right, your knees to the left.

Drop your knees to the sides on the floor and stretch your legs out in front of you and to the sides.

Bring your legs to the center 1 at a time and turn all the way over in a rolling movement with the upper part of your body lifted.

2. Sit with your left leg close to your body flat on the floor, knee bent. Cross it with your right leg (illus. 214). Turn your upper body away from the right leg as far as possible toward the left. Practice this twist to each side.

Standing

1. Alternately push your right and left shoulder forward. Touch your hands lightly to your thighs as you do it.

2. Slowly move your upper body forward and backward and drop into a horizontal (table top) position, with straight back (illus. 215).

Do the same thing while sitting. Go from lying on your back into a sitting position and then return to lying on your back.

Move forward to a count of 3, doing an opposing movement with your shoulders on every step. When the emphasis is on Beat 1, make your shoulder movement more pronounced than on the next 2 beats (see Jazz Walks, Chapter 5).

Shake your shoulders rapidly, 1 at a time, letting your forearms hang loosely.

Practice shoulder shakes in place as you shift your weight and your upper body forward, backward and to the side.

Practice shoulder shakes with your arms raised, elbows and forearms at shoulder level. Turn your head as you move.

Walking

1. Standing in a straddle position, twist your upper body. Then, in a series of jazz walks, make emphasized opposing movements with your shoulders and pelvis.

Project your left shoulder with emphasis during a step to the right.

2. Do the same thing with long running steps, your arms accenting the opposing movement (illus. 212).

3. With back rounded and knees bent, do the same movements, raising or lowering your head. Your shoulders oppose your steps.

In a 3-count, step forward, backward, and bring your feet together. When you put your right foot forward, project your left

214

215

216

shoulder (arms to the side). Turn your upper body toward the step (illus. 216). Do the same thing to the opposite side.

4. Do the same walk, kicking your legs as you twist with opposing movements.

5. Standing on a slightly bent leg, kick your free leg to the side, forward, diagonally, or to the rear. Turn your shoulders and your arms toward your free leg.

Cross your free leg behind the other leg and move your body and arms in the same direction as your free leg.

6. Try the same thing using different rhythms:

Step-kick

Cross your free leg in front of the other leg. Jump onto it. Turn your body rapidly in the opposite direction of the kick. Swing your arms along horizontally.

Step-step-kick

Here the kick is done to 1 side only.

Step-step-step-kick

Here kicking is done alternately to left and right.

Syncopated

Talk out the rhythm: *long-long-long-short-long*

Hopping with Opposing Movements

The basic pattern is step-step-hop.

1. When you hop, extend your leg up and forward. Bend your upper body toward your free leg. Extend your arms to the rear.

2. Swing your free leg to the side. Stretch your upper body sideways toward that free leg (illus. 220). You can hold your arms as an extension of your body, or move them sideways in the opposite direction.

3. Swing your free leg backward, turning your shoulders away from it (illus. 217). Emphasize the opposition with your arms.

217

218

219

220

4. When you hop, bend your free leg at the knee and lift it in front of you or behind you. Twist your shoulders toward that leg (illus. 218).

Lean your upper body back. Swing your arms diagonally up and to the sides (illus. 219).

Explore other variations.

Jumps with Opposing Movements

These are all jumps with opposing twists (see Jazz Jumps, Chapter 5).

1. Do a series of running jumps, turning your body toward the jumping leg, with arms down and to the sides.

2. Do a sideways horse jump, starting from a cross-legged position and landing in it.

3. Starting with a rounded back, knees bent, jump with a knee twist in the air (illus. 221 and 222).

Shoulders and Arms in Opposing Directions

1. Make semi-circles with your shoulders in opposite directions. Let your arms hang down relaxed.

2. Do the same thing with your arms out to the sides, 1 shoulder rolling forward while your entire arm turns with it, palm up (thumb to the rear). Turn your other shoulder toward the rear; that palm also faces up with the thumb back.

Each move starts from the shoulder joints (illus. 223).

3. Combine the twisting of your shoulders with a contraction and release of your chest. Add a sideways movement of your chest.

224

221   222   223

4. Combine the twisting of your shoulders with sideways and crossed steps.

5. Lying on your stomach, turn your shoulders. Keep your arms at your sides, palms on the floor. Turn first your right, then your left shoulder.

Extend this movement with variations (illus. 224).

225

Jazz Falls

Falling movements in jazz dance are rapid transitions from standing or jumping into a position sitting or lying on the floor. You continue the sequence on the floor through the levels and back into a standing position. Simple combinations, artistic combinations and acrobatic ones are part of every jazz dancer's repertoire.

The falls that follow start easily and get more difficult. Practice them on mats at first and then transfer them to the floor. But from the start, dance them with music, first with a slow tempo and then more rapidly.

Falling Exercises

1. Falling Forward

Take a running step forward, slip into a kneeling position (supporting yourself on your knees) and slide flatly forward until you are lying on your stomach.

2. Falling Sideways

From a running step sideways, place your right knee on the floor. Roll over your right shoulder until you are lying on your side. Now do it to the left.

3. Falling Backward

From a standing position, round your back, bend your knees, and (with or without the support of your hands) roll down until you are lying on your back.

Movement Patterns with Falls

Do the falls in a continuous flowing sequence of movement, slowly or rapidly.

Experiment with forward, sideways and backward falls. Can you fall to the floor in a flowing soft way without hurting yourself? Can you do it gracefully, without a sound?

Actually, a fall is a relaxation exercise in which you release tension in a flowing way in 1 part of your body after the other,

starting from your legs. When you lie down, your body should be as relaxed as possible. As you straighten up, you reverse the process.

Practice falling and straightening up with restful music in 8, 6, 4, and 2 beats. When the rhythm speeds up, the gliding movement becomes a falling movement.

1. Combine falling backward with standing up, leading with your side.

2. Start with a running step forward; "fall" into lying on your stomach; roll over onto your back and stand up again.

3. Do a sideways fall to your right and stand, leading with your left side.

4. Practice the falls without using your hands, but keep your body close to the floor.

With a partner

Try falling and standing up where one partner jumps over the other (see pages 97 and 98).

Practice the falls using longer or shorter musical sequences.

With a group

Practice the falls in a group in a sequence of simultaneous movements or as a chain reaction – one movement after the other. Do the same thing straightening up.

Improvise in pairs and in small groups, exploring new possibilities of movement (illus. 225).

226

Falls and Levels

These patterns are more difficult.

1. Do a sequence: from walking, to walking on your knees, to walking erect again (illus. 226).

2. With a 4-count, walk upright, round your back and bend your knees, and then when you are very low, change to a kneeling position with 2 slides on your knees. Proceed forward through the deeply knee-bent position, ending in erect walking (4 beats twice).

3. Do this in 4 beats as before, but when you arrive at the step-kneeling position, sit sideways toward the left next to your knees.

Use your hands to support your body behind your buttocks. Turn further toward the left, making a full turn, and through your right knee, stand up.

4. Stand with your feet separated but parallel to each other (straddle position). Half turn your upper body to the right. Cross your right leg over the left and drop down into a seated position through your left knee.

Fall onto your back, stretching your legs up briefly (illus. 232). Stand by crossing your left leg over your right knee. End with a spread jump.

5. Start from a standing or rounded knee-bent position and jump with

both legs (illus. 227). When you land, bend your knees deeply, round your back and sink into a seated position (illus. 228). Pushing back, end up with your legs stretched out in front of you (illus. 229).

Move backward in that position by alternately drawing your legs out from the hip to the right and to the left (illus. 230). Work your arms at angles in opposing swings. Stand by drawing up both lower legs until you are kneeling and then rise, one leg at a time, without using your hands (illus. 231).

6. From a knee-bent position with your right leg out to the side, kneel on your left knee and roll

227

228   229   230   231

232

sideways over your right shoulder, onto your right side. Then extend your left leg, draw your right leg up, then your left leg, and walk on your knees into a sideways bent position, and stand.

7. Do the same thing, but start with a jump to the right. Land with your weight on your left leg and then continue as before.

8. Do it again, but this time start with a jump to the left, from a crossed-foot position.

9. Do a half-turn as you jump. Then walk with your buttocks drawn back. Fall backward and roll onto your back. After a shoulder roll backward, stand by walking on your knees.

10. Standing, kick back 1 leg as you jump onto your hands on the floor (illus. 233 and 234). The instep of your standing leg helps to support your body. Then lie flat on your stomach, roll over lengthwise, and using your forearms for support, draw your knees under your body.

Stretch out again (illus. 235) and draw into a kneeling position like a worm (illus. 236). Then move into a rounded, deeply bent position and do a turning jump into a spiral-shaped straightening up.

233 234

235 236

237 238 239

240

241

242

11. Be sure to try this on a mat. Swing your legs up (illus. 237), catching yourself with a handstand. (illus. 238). Release, lower your shoulders and roll through your chest onto your stomach (illus. 239), or into the kneeling position again.

Finish in any form you've already tried, or find a new way to rise.

12. Jazz fall to the side in combination
From a standing position, push your right hip out to the right (illus. 240) and fall toward the right, crossing your left leg in front of your right during the fall (illus. 241), and making a quarter turn toward the right.

Catch the fall with both hands, your left knee supporting you, your right leg extended (illus. 242).

243

244

Move your right leg into a kneeling position, raise your back up bent, doing a $\frac{3}{4}$ turn to the right on your left knee. Use your hand to help you shift in the turn (illus. 243) and end up looking toward the front, as you were at the start.

Now put your right knee down, and stand slowly, snapping your fingers (illus. 244).

245

246

247

With a partner
Do this fall in different directions.

13. Sideways fall onto your side.
Start as before (illus. 245), but after
crossing your left leg in front of
your right, roll over onto your right
side – first with your knee, then
with your hip (illus. 246), and
lastly with your shoulder (illus. 247).
Then roll over onto your back,
draw your knee to your chest, and
continue rolling onto your knees,
while your upper body lies flat on
the floor. When your knees are
under you, stand through the
kneeling walk, or jump into a deeply
bent position.

Rising – Variations

From a kneeling position, but with
your body erect, move both arms
toward the right and then swing
them rapidly toward the left. As
you swing them, move your body
into a deeply bent, rounded back
position, and jump onto your left
foot, holding your right leg free to
the side (illus. 248). Draw up your
right leg and put down your foot
while you turn further toward the
left (illus. 249) and straighten up.

From the floor, do a half turn to
the right into the lying position,
and with both hands to support
you, jump into a walking position,
making a half turn to the left.

248   249

250   251

252   253

95

254

14. From a jazz run (illus. 250), slide through a brief split position (illus. 251) into a hurdle position. Use your left hand as a support and extend your right arm upward.

After a full turn to the right on the floor (illus. 252 and 253), stand up through the knee-walk. Do the whole sequence in 16 beats accompanied by fast music.

15. Jazz fall backward
From a narrow sideways straddle, push your knees and pelvis forward. Let your extended body sink backward with your right arm over your head, an extension of your shoulder (illus. 254). Straighten your bent knees slowly and slide your upper body backward (illus. 255) until you are lying flat on your back (illus. 256).

255

256

It's a good idea to practice this with the help of a partner (illus. 257) who holds your left arm as you fall backward (illus. 258).

With a partner
Do the backward jazz fall in different directions (illus. 259-261).

257

258

259

260

261

262

7 Improvisation in Jazz Dance

Solo — with a Partner — and in a Group

Improvisation in Jazz Dance

Solo – with a Partner – and in a Group

Improvisation is basic to all jazz. Improvisation means playing with a theme, spontaneous free expression. You can improvise at any stage of your training, even when you're just starting to learn basic forms.

Improvisation in dance also means testing and experimenting with your own body, with movements, with music, with rhythm, with space and with concepts, ideas and emotions. What is important in improvisation is not so much creative freedom as it is connection to your subject, working it out with concentration and completeness.

Start out by stating the subject of your improvisation in jazz style – even if you're not fluent in jazz technique. As you work, the techniques you've learned will flow in. As your ability increases, your improvisations will become more interesting and varied.

Themes for Improvisation

Subjects for improvisations come from various ideas:

Movement patterns
Forms in space
Rhythms
Music
Imagination
Communication games

Improvisations Based on Movement Patterns

1. Let's say your improvisation is to explore all kinds of jazz hopping. Working alone, you can experiment with the hops you know – step hops, gallops, and so on – and adapt them to the music. Try to find new hops and improvise in new paths, with different tempos.

2. Theme: the pattern of run-run-hop. Play with this movement pattern alone, with a partner, or with new partners from the group. Here you can use all kinds of jazz runs and hops. Vary them using other techniques you've learned. You can change the direction of movement, perform entire sections in a bent position, stay in 1 spot or use lots of space.

Expand the hop into a jump, intensifying it rhythmically.

3. Theme: jazz turns. Be sure to select music which provides a stimulus for your theme. In this case, for example, if you don't choose music which is suitable for turning, everyone might turn continuously without being able to interrupt the flow of movement. Don't turn in only 1 direction so that you get dizzy, but vary your turns. Start slowly and don't turn rapidly for too long.

Use different levels: high and low down to the floor, and when you're there, continue to turn. Include your arms, head and body in the turning.

With a partner
You can vary the turning movements by:
    holding hands differently
    alternating turns, with 1 person
        moving around the other
    taking inside and outside
        positions with a third person

4. Theme: Head Isolation
You can put the idea into a kind of story. In this case, everyone might move about, and then spontaneously stand in front of a partner. Both partners might make head movements – nodding, shaking turning, or circling – and then proceed to a new partner. The music can determine the sequence: for example, milling about for 8 steps, and making head move-ments in front of a partner for 8 beats.

Partners might promenade through the room, looking toward and away from each other. You could make it into a satiric play, adding mimicry and gestures.

Standing in pairs, one partner might make slow varied head movements, with the other imitating them rapidly.

264

5. Theme: Shoulder Isolation
Here you'd move your shoulders actively with all the other parts of your body following passively – relaxed. You could do it in place – crouching or kneeling or standing – and then walking.

You might kneel next to or in front of a partner, both of you trying to make contact through shoulder movements. Find ideas in common and develop them into a definite sequence of movement. Try the same thing standing and moving.

In a group improvisation, one person could stand in front of the group and in a "Simon-Says" of shoulder movement, the group would follow that lead.

Or 2 groups could stand opposite each other and carry on a wordless "conversation" which can also express emotions (agreement, snobbery, excitement).

Improvisations Based on Forms in Space

Divide the room with rectangular lines. Everyone does jazz walks in these lines with quarter turns (illus. 265).

The dancers should move independently, but they should keep aware of the space distribution so that there are no collisions or traffic jams.

You can move backward or to the the side, if necessary.

In this improvisation, the number of steps in 1 direction is set ahead of time. Everybody turns at the same time after 2, 3, 4 or 8 steps. Be sure to choose appropriate music!

Variation: Try the same exercise on diagonals, always facing 1 corner of the room (illus. 266).

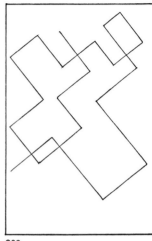

266

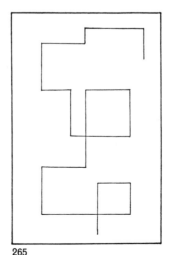

265

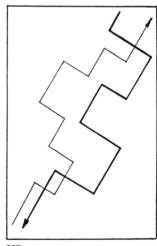

267

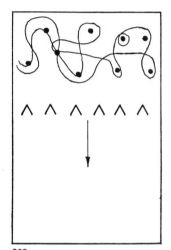

268

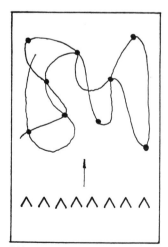

269

You might travel the same paths in pairs, next to each other and behind each other, with 1 of you determining the direction.

Or do the same thing in small groups, each group moving with quarter turns through the room, 1 person leading and providing the direction.

Two groups might approach each other and change sides. You can change your design so that groups come from 4 corners (illus. 267).

The lead can switch with each change in direction. The person who is in front takes the lead.(First practice this in pairs!)

If your group likes this, try it with with definite setups. Then it won't be an improvisation anymore, but part of a composition.

You can try another design: widening and narrowing the room with 2 groups. One group moves around in 1 section of the room like a swarm of mosquitoes. Then the other group advances in a single line. The room for the "mosquitoes" becomes narrower and narrower. The mosquito group should keep moving around each other at the same tempo, even though the room is becoming smaller. They need to adapt the

length of the steps they take to keep the tempo constant (illus. 268). Then, as the "line" retreats with large steps, the swarm of mosquitoes immediately re-occupies the newly won space (illus. 269).

You can make this into a play that has to do with war, aggression, survival.

Improvisations Based on Rhythm

1. Theme: Drum Beats
Your whole body can play this. Use polyrhythmic (several rhythms at the same time) African drum music.

You could start with your hands drumming on the floor, but drums are standing all around in your imagination. Lying on your stomach and your back, crouching and standing up, you can drum out rhythms that go with the music or against it.

You can drum with your feet, with your hands and feet at the same time, in a deeply bent position and upright. Your arms can drum on your thighs or you can clap your hands.

2. Theme: Any particular rhythm, such as 1-2-3.

270

Find various movements for it. You can emphasize the rhythm by finger snapping, stamping and clapping. For example, in 3/4 rhythm:

Beat 1: right-hand snap
Beat 2 and 3: 2 left-hand snaps

or

Beat 1: clap your hands
Beat 2: 2 right-hand slaps on your right thigh
Beat 3: 3 left-hand slaps on the left thigh

Combination: Put them all together:

Right snap
Left snap snap
Clap
Right slap slap
Left slap slap slap

You might work out variations like these with claps and snaps and stamps and slaps. Two partners or 2 groups could clap the rhythm alternately. Your feet could take over the rhythm and walk it. You could represent it in space with a zigzag line.

If you have 2 groups working simultaneously with different themes, 1 group could clap and stamp in place while the other group translates the rhythm into movement.

You could give individual themes to the dancers and then combine them into an overall composition (see Choreography, Chapter 8).

Improvisations Based on Music

When you're improvising to music, you can choose the rhythm, melody, dynamics, repetitions (structure) and expression (mood) of the music you want to express in movement.

Try moving against the music or in contrast to it.

Improvisations Based on Imagination

1. Theme: Skating
You can take long sliding steps with samba music. Your arms might accompany the skating. Experiment: What can you do on skates? Turn, jump, glide, fall – do all of it.

You can use soft round curved lines, bend deeply with hip movements and opposing twists.

2. Theme: Play Statue Tag
You might begin the game without music and then continue it with music. What changes?

Stylize the game to make it a dance:

A few dancers are catchers and run through the room with long jazz-like steps. Everyone touched by the gentle (more indicated than actual) touch becomes a statue – enchanted in a bizarre position – until he or she is released again by gentle contact with a free runner.

This is a wonderful way to experiment with the theme of tension-relaxation.

3. Theme: Statue Tag as Pantomime

Three people start the catching game first without music. Then, accompanied by jazz music, they act out the catching in groups of 3. One of the 3 follows the other 2 as the catcher. They act out the rapid running, the escape, the touching with an extended arm. The pantomime can also express the fear of being followed, the terror of being touched, the joy of being captured.

4. Theme: Basketball
Groups of 3 to 5, in stylized movements, pantomime throwing a ball, catching, passing, dribbling, throwing it into the basket, attacking and defending.

You can do other games the same way – soccer, volleyball, football, hockey – in small groups.

271

Improvisations Based on Communication Games

1. Theme: Trust

One partner closes his or her eyes and stands passive and relaxed. He or she will react to what the active partner does. Let's say the active partner shakes the hand and arm of the passive one. The passive partner submits completely to these movements, keeping as relaxed and yielding as possible. The active partner might use both hands to turn the passive one's head to the right and left, turn his or her body, push it, guide it.

Be sure to change rôles!

2. Theme: Chain Formation

Form a chain of 5 to 7 dancers, extending hands to form a circle or a line. The goal: to move jointly in the room to music without letting go. But meanwhile, each person in the group needs to experiment with the positions possible while still holding hands (illus. 272).

The circle can grow larger and smaller. Interweavings will take place when dancers turn and cross their arms, especially if they slip under the clasped hands or climb over them!

Choose a lively rhythm so that the group can maintain a light running movement.

3. Theme: Instant Imitation

Everyone forms a large circle. One person moves into the center in a particular style of movement. Then everyone imitates that movement, doing it in exactly the same way.

As a basic pattern, use 4 or 8 beats going into the circle and the same coming out of it.

You can vary this, with 1 person inventing a new form and presenting it to the group alone in the center of the circle. Then everyone repeats it 3 times (4 beats for the solo dancer, 12 beats for the rest).

If the improvisation is very successful and you want to move fast, let the group repeat the form only once and have a new presentation dancer start immediately. This requires concentration, quick reactions on the part of the group, as well as spontaneous action on the part of the individual.

272

8 Choreography, Composition & Jazz Dance

Choreography, Composition & Jazz Dance

Jazz compositions can be designed by 1 person (a choreographer), or you can invent them jointly.

Using a single choreographer may be more efficient, but there are advantages in working out compositions jointly. In the course of this creation, some individuals emerge with more abundant and interesting ideas than you'd ever expect.

Ways to Start

From movement themes and finding the right music

From the music, and putting together the movements you want

From the content – ideas, imagination, feelings, and finding the music and movement patterns you want

Movement Themes

Take movement themes you develop during improvisations and combine them harmoniously by inventing transitions between them.

You can start from themes of movement such as:

1. Isolation movements of the centers
Groups can perform them simultaneously or one at a time or both.

2. Tension-relaxation, contraction-release, or falls and levels

3. Basic forms, such as jazz walks, runs, hops, jumps

4. Combined jazz dance forms which contain a little of everything.

274

275

Music Themes

Music which is suitable for movement stimulates compositions. It is natural to translate it into dance. First, listen to the music over and over. Immerse yourself in it. Then start by improvising movements.

Be sure to:
1. Analyze the music: Make note of the time units (4/4, 3/4, 7/8, time changes).

2. Pick out the musical motifs which recur and to which movement motifs will correspond.

3. Note repetitions, intensifications, high points, and closings, first by memory and later graphically as well.

4. Listen for the peculiarities of a piece of music, its accents, its dissonant sounds, syncopations, changes in time, and tempo, phrasings, dynamics. You need to take all of them into consideration in developing a dance.

Music does not always have to be "interpreted." In jazz, it's also possible to move *against* the rhythm (in a syncopated way). In the case

of polyrhythmics (several rhythms running together), everyone can pick out his or her own individual rhythm.

If you choose music that lacks high points, you can give it accents and high points with movement alone. In this case, however, the music becomes merely a rhythmic, melodic background to the dance.

The music you select determines the character of your creation. You can take music from all modern fields – pop, disco, rock and roll, Dixieland, country music, African

276

277

278

and South American folklore, Latin rhythms, jazzed up folk and jazzed up classics, depending on your taste, your personal feeling for the music and its degee of difficulty.

Content Themes

Mental images, ideas, pictures and feelings can be translated into dance movement. This type of dance is called expressive, idea or action dance.

Show music is particularly easy to choreograph expressively. For example:

1. *Porgy and Bess*
Content: An individual is the dance leader and gets the group to dance. The mood is happy, light, humorous.

2. *West Side Story*
Content: 2 groups feud and dance opposing each other. Mood: provocative, aggressive.

3. *Jesus Christ Superstar*
Content: A large group dances around a single person, praying, honoring, praising. Mood: jubilation, mystic surrender, ecstasy.

Most musical plays and musical comedies have dramatic themes which you can use to create simple jazz dance compositions. It's best to have the group select the theme and the music.

General Principles in Jazz Choreography

Structure of a Composition

The structure of a jazz composition can be extremely varied. It is not a sequence of jazz motifs, but rather a musical, dancing, and expressive composition which should have 1 or more high points, and end with a definite conclusion. The conclusion can be a gradual withdrawal into the background or a simple subsiding, perhaps, with a slow sinking to the floor. Or you may want to close on a high point or a surprise effect. This structure will depend upon the music.

279

Developing Movement in Jazz Compositions

The important thing in composing movement motifs is the development of the movement. A successful composition may be abrupt, with a multiplicity of new movements, but it is more likely to grow from variations and nuances, to develop, 1 form from the others, all of them contributing to a harmonious whole.

Repetition makes a great impression on the dancers and on the spectators, but too frequent repetition gets monotonous. Instead of straight repetition, modify the motifs and vary them. Introduce changes of rhythm and tempo. Limit or expand the movement. Switch the direction. Make different use of space. Let different groups take over the motifs. You can practice these principles even with simple basic forms.

Rhythmic Differentiation

Jazz dance is inspired by rhythmic-dynamic music. The rhythm of the music corresponds to movement impulses in the centers of our bodies.

In a composition, the rhythm should alternate dynamically between the high points and the subsiding elements, between the explosive and the reserved sequences. The rhythm should slow down and accelerate; quicken into half time or double-time for a movement; syncopate; oppose itself; pause, hesitate, and accentuate – by clapping, finger-snapping, stamping, tapping the heels and balls of your feet, even yelling and making other noises! If you choose, you can add rhythmic accents with musical devices such as drums, sticks. or rattles.

Composition and Space— Choreography

Choreography is created when you set down the dancers' directions and movements in space. You are permitting fleeting images to appear in 3-dimensions.

You can work with forms such as blocks, rows, lines, alleys and circles, which are easy to see – this is especially useful when you're choreographing folk and group dances. Asymmetric images – and constant reformation of group structures – are characteristic of jazz choreography. The directions and paths move apart and converge. Groupings cause moments of tension as they form and break up. The dynamic alternation between these rapidly moving groups produces exciting, exhilarating effects.

Examples of Choreographic Group Arrangements

A single person may oppose a group (illus. 280).

280

A few may oppose many (illus. 281).

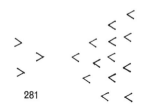

281

Several individuals may move in various directions (illus. 282).

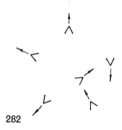

282

Several small groups may oppose each other (illus. 283).

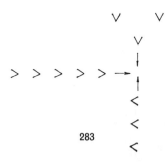

283

Groups may be of various sizes (illus. 284).

284

and various shapes (illus. 285).

285

Dance Radiance

A composition which intends to be a dance must have "dance radiance." It must have an infectious, stimulating effect on the people dancing it and on the people watching it. Sometimes it is simply this radiance which makes the difference between jazz gymnastics and jazz dance.

If your composition has a content theme, it should transmit the message in mood and in expression to the people watching it. This is more difficult when you're working with abstract ideas. You may want to make the ideas clearer through oral or written explanations.

The individual dancer, even when working within a group, should express his or her individual power of radiance. Even in the case of a movement sequence where everyone does the same thing, there should be room for individuality and personal expression.

286

287

288

289

290

9 Teaching Jazz Dance

Teaching Jazz Dance

In the course of our cultural history, the importance of dance has been downgraded. We no longer use it in religious ritual. It seldom plays a part in community celebrations. We don't teach it in school. It has become a leisure time occupation. But now with leisure time increasing, dance is beginning to come back into its own. Many schools are becoming aware of the need to promote dance as an activity along with sport and play. The "dance gap" in school needs to be filled, just as it is for art and crafts, shop, and other activities.

Most jazz dance training traditionally starts at about 13 or 14 years old, but that is already too late. At 11 and 12, young people are freer, and more interested in the acrobatic aspects of jazz dance, too.

But how about younger children? How do 4-10-year-olds react to jazz? Do they have the ability to do it? This age group (both boys and and girls) are ideally suited to start jazz and disco dancing. They have an easier time exploring fantasy, and take joy in their movements. They are looser, less inhibited. They are quite capable of experimenting with basic gymnastic forms – walking, running, hopping, springing, swinging and turning –

and love to do it, especially to jazz and disco music. They can easily practice isolating the individual body centers through loose shaking, circular free movements (even preschoolers). They can also practice tension-release, even though the more difficult coordinations (such as polycentrics and step combinations) are beyond them.

Over the years, dance training has been considered feminine, and boys have had to do without it. But boys and girls dance the same way in their free time. Jazz and disco dancing are made up of of couples – pairs of the sexes – proving that boys and girls of all ages can learn dance together.

Jazz in Education

Jazz dance training provides immensely valuable educational experiences. It develops creativity at every stage, as students translate concepts, feelings, and fantasy into their own personal styles of movement. It encourages spontaneous expression, as they learn to allow the beat of the music, a partner, a verbal command, to call forth an immediate response. It increases sensitivity, as the dancer empathises with a partner, with the group – even with a rhythm, movement or style – and flexibility, both mental and physical.

In small or large groups, this training develops individuality, as students work out their own dance forms. It teaches them how to work together, as they practice, improvise and compose. They learn self-discipline, how to tolerate criticism and how to dish it out – constructively. They learn how to set and accomplish short and long-term goals, from mastering a tricky coordination to building a production number.

Who Should Teach It?

As a jazz dance teacher, you don't need to be a gym teacher. You can teach the class as long as you're thoroughly acquainted with dance techniques, practically as well as theoretically. Only when you become acquainted with the disco style or jazz, and have practiced it yourself, can you transmit it to the students convincingly.

Age does not play an important part in this. The important things are the style and technique of movement which you need to master. Much of the fascination of jazz and disco dancing is due to the intense physical movement and the joyful feeling you get when you do it. As a jazz and disco teacher, you have a vital job: You express – and show others how to express – freedom and joy.

About Uta Fischer-Munstermann

For the last 15 years, Uta Fischer-Munstermann has been teaching dance, pantomime and various gymnastic systems to students of all ages and to physical education teachers.

Known in Germany and abroad for her adult classes and her teacher-training courses, she has also published articles in journals in the fields of dance and gymnastics, as well as several books. Ms. Munstermann is particularly interested in African dance and jazz dance, their stylistic directions and expressive forms. She has studied African movement with dance historian, Helmut Guenther, of Stuttgart, the leading authority in the field. Ms. Munstermann performs dance demonstrations with her own dance group, many of which have developed into artistic, successful theatrical productions.

Ms. Munstermann studied with Mary Wigman in Berlin (expressionist dance); with Maja Lex; with Rose Daiber (elementary dance); with Anneliese Schmolke (folklore and rhythm theatre); and has worked with Brigitte Trommler in Munich (contemporary dance and choreography).

About Liz Williamson

Award-winning dancer, choreographer and researcher, Liz Williamson is an international jazz teacher who teaches dance on all levels—beginner to professional. She headed the dance department of the Dalton School in New York City for several years and has taught as artist-in-residence at colleges and universities in the U.S.A. and Canada. She has been guest artist and teacher in France; Belgium; Rio de Janeiro, Brazil; Quebec, Canada, and at dance festivals in both East and West Germany.

She was the recipient of the Elsa Heilich Kempe award for her contribution and dedication to the art of dance, and she has performed on stage as a solo dancer as well as with the Alvin Ailey Company and others on television and in films.

She has published a history of jazz dance from its African origins to the present time.

Index